Baghdad

THE BRADT CITY GUIDE

Catherine Arnold

Bradt Travel Guides Ltd, UK
The Globe Pequot Press Inc, USA

First published September 2004

Bradt Travel Guides Ltd, 19 High Street, Chalfont St Peter, Bucks SL9 9QE, England
Published in the USA by The Globe Pequot Press Inc, 246 Goose Lane, PO Box 480,
Guilford, Connecticut 06437-0480

Text copyright © 2004 Catherine Arnold
Maps copyright © 2004 Bradt Travel Guides Ltd
Map source material provided by ESR Cartography Ltd and ITMB

British Library Cataloguing in Publication Data
A catalogue record for this book is available from the British Library

ISBN-10: 1 84162 097 1
ISBN-13: 978 1 84162 097 8

Photographs
Front cover Mustansiriya School (Catherine Arnold) *Text* Geoff Hann (GH), Catherine Arnold (CA)
Maps Steve Munns *Illustrations* C Hassall, Carole Vincer
Typeset from the author's disc by Wakewing
Printed and bound in Spain by Grafo SA, Bilbao

Author

Born in Pusan, South Korea, Catherine Arnold grew up in Korea, Egypt, the UAE and Sri Lanka before moving to the Isle of Wight when she was 16. After graduating from Trinity College, Cambridge, she completed an MPhil in Philosophy of Religion and continues to be fascinated by the influence of religion on modern thought, society and world affairs.

In June 2003, Catherine took up a position as staff writer on the *Baghdad Bulletin*, an independent news magazine based in Iraq. While in Baghdad she also wrote for magazines and newspapers in the UK, USA and the Middle East and was regularly invited to comment on the situation in Baghdad for network radio and TV in the UK and USA.

DISCLAIMER

Visitors to Baghdad must remain vigilant at all times and informed on both the current situation in the city and any area they wish to visit therein. Mention of sites, tours and day trips does not constitute a security endorsement. It is essential that any visitor be fully appraised of the current risks before embarking on any purely pleasurable excursion within the city, and that such trips be avoided altogether while any question remains as to the safety of doing so.

Contents

Contents

Contents

Acknowledgements

Whenever I open a book to find acknowledgements one thought always flashes through my mind: surely the only person who ever reads to the end is the person who can't find his or her name. Unfortunately the many people who have helped inform, prod, cajole and defend both author and book, cannot begin to fit on one page, but without a few the book could never have been written. The first thank you must therefore go to the indefatigable Wisam Akram and Esam Pasha, who spent endless sweaty days touring around the city and many more answering a barrage of questions. Then to Ralph Hassall for reading every word and keeping it up-to-date. Thanks also by name to James Brandon for lengthy responses (when they didn't involve chicken), Wissam al-Atrakhji for dining at numerous restaurants (involving chicken), my parents Ernest and Pamela Arnold for living without a phone for months and to all those who helped at the IAC and Ministry of Culture. Also David Enders, Piers Drysdale, Shadi al-Qassem and the Bradt team.

I'm grateful to those who kindly agreed to write boxes – if you read the book you'll know who they are, and the friends who kept me entertained while in Baghdad – if they're reading this they'll know who they are! Then there are always beginnings. I'm grateful both to the *Baghdad Bulletin* for getting me to Iraq in the first place and to Luke Baker for suggesting me as someone mad enough to consider wandering round the streets of a war-torn city looking for antiquities and good restaurants.

If it is you – be assured that I am most certainly grateful and have not forgotten.

IRAQ AT A GLANCE

Location An ancient cross-road with Jordan and Syria to the west, Saudi Arabia to the south, Turkey to the north and Iran to the east. 58km of coast in the south.

Size 437,072km^2

Climate Cold winters, extremely hot summers

Time GMT + 3 hours, GMT + 4 daylight saving (April 1–October 1)

International dialling code +964

Currency Iraqi Dinar ID1,500–2,000 = US$1 app

Population 25,374,691 (July 2004 est)

Population growth per year 2.74% (2004 est)

Life expectancy in years at birth 67.09 male, 69.48 female (2004 est)

Infant mortality 55.16 deaths/1,000 live births

Capital Baghdad, population around 5.6 million

Baghdad GPS location 33.21n 44.25e, elevation: 34m

Ethnicity Arab 75–80%, Kurd 15–20%, other (Turkomen, Assyrian, others) 5%

Language Arabic (Iraqi dialect), Kurdish, Assyrian, Armenian, English

Religion 97% Muslim (Shia 60–65%, Sunni 32–37%), 3% Christian and other (includes Jewish, Yazidi and Sabaeans)

Introduction

When I first arrived in Baghdad in June 2003, it was to find a city in collective shock. There were elements of optimism, there was the feeling that maybe this was the start of something new, that a terrible dictator had finally gone, but three wars, ten years of sanctions and several weeks of debauched looting seemed to have destroyed something deeper than the infrastructure of the city: the population was in a daze and afraid.

Working for the *Baghdad Bulletin*, the first English-language news magazine to be published after the fall of Baghdad, my fellow colleagues and I were privy to an almost unique perspective of the situation over those first, faltering months after the fall of Saddam Hussein. While the rest of the Western community were housed in the relative safety of hotels or fortress-like houses, generators throbbing, finances forced us into the community. We worried about looters, sat up with our neighbours through the night, AK47 to hand, sweated through the long, dark evenings without power, went days without a shower when the water failed, tiptoed through the rising pool of sewage that had formed down our middle-class street and joined in the communal outrage when the owner of the local alcohol stall was shot in broad daylight by a car full of armed youths.

We watched as the temperature soared, tempers rising in sympathy. Apathy was turning into anger. Petrol queues snaked into the shimmering distance, traffic chaos turned simple journeys into three-hour battles, high on the choking black fumes that turned to mud on sweaty faces. Honest drivers faced the indignity of private security guards screaming at them in a foreign tongue, pistols pointed at their chest, their only crime to be stuck in a gridlock when someone important needed to pass. The small-windowed, low-ceilinged houses built for air conditioning became intolerable ovens and the restless population of Baghdad spent endless, sleepless nights on mattresses rotten with sweat and sheets stained an oily yellow. Resentment turned to rage.

We also heard, unsanitised, the daily tragedies that fanned the anger. Of elderly mothers gasping their last breaths in a fetid pool of sweat, of children killed by falling bullets or babies dying in intensive care for want of diesel to run the generators, and of young men spattered with bullets at checkpoints.

Of course there was the other side too. We donned our sweaty finest to talk to NGOs and CPA workers, many of whom were, and still are, banging their heads against the concrete barriers, frustrated by bureaucracy and security concerns in their attempts to rebuild Iraq, with many risking and some losing their lives to rebuild the country.

We went to press conferences for Western journalists and could smile at the often inflated hours of electricity being fed to the generator-soothed press corps. Maybe somewhere in the city they'd had 16 hours of power, but it wasn't where we lived, nor where any of our translators lived, all of us increasingly black-eyed from lack of sleep.

We spoke to the soldiers, boys-next-door on their first trip from home, baffled, not quite understanding why the Iraqi people didn't love them when they were here to help. Increasingly petrified, but with a stock of stories to last them a lifetime, if they ever got to live it. One of my favourite stories was of a community-action initiative tasked with cleaning up a village outside Baghdad. A group of older children had been caught stealing and the punishment was to bury the rubbish collected by soldiers and workers. The soldier couldn't help noticing that these mischievous, perky children seem suddenly cowed, then the first began to cry and soon all of them were sobbing over their spades. Having deliberately given them a lenient task he was nonplussed and went in search of a translator. The explanation was simple; they had assumed they were digging their graves.

Returning to Baghdad in November, I found a different city. Some progress had been made, but the most pronounced change was the attitude of the people. The cool winter breezes had genuinely calmed tempers. Arguments for or against the Coalition presence were rationalised and optimism and pessimism well thought out, sometimes with an icy reasoning more disheartening or frightening than the previous knee-jerk responses. Meanwhile barriers twice the height of a man had sprung up, forming impregnable phalanxes of concrete around any potential target. Roads were blocked off and the 'Baghdad frot' had become a ubiquitous rite of passage. An impenetrable physical divide had been set up between the locals and those there to help them.

Looking back, however, one thing stands out and that is the extraordinary generosity of the people. Baghdadis, no matter how little they have for themselves,

Introduction

are overflowing with hospitality and eager to help. Our cook with a young family to support tried to give one of us $100 after a theft left us short of cash. It was more than her month's wage. This may be an extreme example but the meals, the unasked-for errands and the chorus of offers of shelter if 'things get bad' were well beyond any call of duty and could easily have placed entire families at risk. Baghdadis seem simply unable to help being generous.

So prepare to enjoy, if not your time in Baghdad, the wonderful people who will populate it. Try to give as you receive and don't forget that, despite the burnt and bombed ruins that surround you, these are a people used to an order and infrastructure as advanced as many Western countries. Remember that Baghdadis find the absence of entertainment, the chaotic traffic, the lack of amenities and the endemic fear even more aggravating than you do, because they can't leave. They are a justifiably proud people, whose city was the capital of the world when London was an overgrown village and Columbus several centuries away from America. War has not destroyed this and Western condescension is met with the scorn it deserves.

DEDICATION

The book is dedicated to my grandmother, Audrey Joan Hudson Murray, who sadly didn't live to worry about me going to Baghdad.

Contents

Over Baghdad is stationed death's loud herald –
Weep for her, then, weep for time's rapine there!
Erstwhile, upon her stream by war imperilled,
When in her streets its flames were briefly bated,
Men hoped her happy fortunes reinstated.
Now all their hopes have turned to dull despair!
Since she, from youth to eldritch death declined,
Hath lost the beauty that once charmed mankind.

Abu Tammam (died 846), quoted by Ibn Battutah in *The Travels of Ibn Battutah* (c1325)

After making the epic journey from the mountains of Turkey where they rise, the Tigris and Euphrates uncurl their way through Iraq, leaving behind two green sweeps of fertility in an otherwise barren desert. Glancing at a map of Iraq, the twin rivers engage in a never-ending dance that sends them whirling away from each other only to be drawn perilously close, flung away once more, and finally united in al-Qurna, believed to be the garden of Eden, their waters mingling in the Shatt al-Arab for the final 190km before disappearing into the Persian Gulf.

In the fertile swathe of land where the two rivers nearly meet, ensuing civilisations have built their capitals, the list tumbling out like a roll-call of ancient history: Kish, where the Sumerian Sun-god Utu (Shamash) lowered Kingship from heaven after the Great Flood; Akkad, seat of Sargon the Great and the fearsome Akkadian Empire; Eshnunna, where tablets of codified law predating that of Hammurabi were inscribed; Babylon, city of Hammurabi, Nebuchadnezzar, the legendary Tower of Babel and home to one of the seven wonders of the world; Dur-Kurigalzu, centre of the Kassite Empire; Seleucia, founded by Seleucus I Nicator, a general under Alexander the Great who made it the base for his ensuing dynasty; Ctesiphon, winter capital of the Parthian and later Sassanid empires; and finally Baghdad, capital of the caliphs and city of a *Thousand and One Nights*.

HISTORY
Timeline

637	Battle of Qadisiya
749	Al-Saffa made first Abbasid Caliph
757	*Offa becomes King of Mercia (central England) issuing gold coins with Arabic inscriptions*
762	Round-city of Baghdad founded by Al-Mansour
775	Harroun Al-Rasheed becomes Caliph
800	*Charlemagne crowned Holy Roman Emperor*
836	Mu'tasim-billah removes the capital to Samarra
838	*Vikings come as far as the walls of Constantinople*
882	Baghdad again becomes the capital
946	Round-city abandoned, Baghdad moves to the eastern bank

Contexts

1015	*Danish King Canute takes control of most of England*
1048	Buyids a Shia dynasty take control of Baghdad
1055	Toghril Beg enters Baghdad and founds the Seljuk dynasty
1066	*Battle of Hastings*
1066	The Seljuks renovate the Imam al-Adham Mosque and Abu Hanifa's Shrine
1118	Mustarshid, 29th Abbasid caliph, regains power from the Seljuks
1202	Sitt Zumurrud Khatun dies and is placed in her mausoleum
1215	*Signing of the Magna Carta*
1225	Sheik Omar al-Sahrawerdi's shrine built
1234	Mustansiriya college completed by Mustansir the penultimate Abbasid caliph
1258	Hulegu, grandson of Jengis Kahn, sacks Baghdad
1289	Construction of the Caliph's Mosque minaret
1357	Khan Mirjan built by the governor of Baghdad Amin-ed-din Mirjan
1387	*Chaucer writes 'Canterbury Tales' (probable date)*
1401	Timurlane launches his final and most devastating attack on Baghdad
1410	Black Sheep Turkman dynasty founded by Qara Yasuf
1470	Black Sheep dynasty overthrown by the White Sheep Turkmen dynasty
1492	*Columbus reaches America*
1508	Shah Ishmael al-Safawi captures Baghdad after overthrowing the White Sheep
1515	Current al-Kadhimain shrine built
1517	*Beginning of the Reformation*
1534	Ottoman Suleiman the Magnificent enters Baghdad

History

1564	*Birth of Shakespeare*
1632	Safavids recapture Baghdad
1638	Safavids ousted from Baghdad by Murad IV the Ottoman sultan
1688	*Parliamentary rule begins in England*
1751	Marmaluk dynasty takes custody of Baghdad for the Ottomans
1776	*US declare Independence*
1817	Daud Pasha becomes governor of Baghdad
1821	*Death of Napoleon*
1830	Bubonic plague ravages Baghdad
1869	Madhat Pasha governs Baghdad introducing reforms, first newspaper printed
1917	Baghdad taken by the British army
1932	Iraq becomes a fully independent state

The build up to Baghdad

In AD637, at the head of an Arab army, Sa'd ibn Abi Aqqas swept down the plain of al-Qadisiya to meet the mighty Sassanid army. Despite the latter's superior numbers and military power that included battle elephants, the Arabs scored a resounding victory. The humiliation of their army sent shockwaves throughout the Sassanid (Persian) Empire and paved the way for its demise only five years later.

Iraq then fell under Islamic control and although the capital of the Umayyad Empire was moved to Damascus from Kufa, Iraq continued to play a powerful political role in a caliphate that at its height stretched from India to Spain.

Contexts

With an economy based on agrarian surplus, expansion eventually burnt out an empire already riven with political and religious conflict. A strong Shia lobby in Iraq believed that only a member of Mohammed's family should rule over the Arab world. This was the perfect opportunity for the Abbasids, who played heavily on their leader's descent from the Prophet's uncle Abbas.

In 749 after the defeat of the Umayyad caliph, Mansour II, at Kufa, al-Saffa was crowned the first Abbasid caliph. The remainder of his brief rule was spent consolidating his newly founded dynasty and shedding the Shia mantle that had brought him to power. His ruthless purging of Umayyads was followed by his brother's equally brutal massacre of the Shia leadership.

It was this brother, Caliph Abu Ja'far al-Mansour, who moved the capital of his empire from al-Anbar to Baghdad in AD762.

The building of Baghdad

The site on which al-Mansour chose to plant his new city had been occupied for millennia. The earliest known reference is found in a legal document dating from the time of Hammurabi (1800BC) that refers to 'Bagdadu'. Ancient boundary stones recovered by archaeologists indicate that it was called Baghdadi under the Kassite king Nazimaruttas (1341–16BC) and Baghdadou at the time of the Babylonian king Mardouk Apalidin (1208–1195BC).

By the time Mansour arrived Baghdad was a collection of small villages clustered around a Nestorian monastery, Dayr al-Atiq, and populated primarily with the descendants of the prisoners and slaves of the Byzantines. The choice of location was strategic: positioned at the crossroads between two worlds (the Orient to the east and the Mediterranean and Europe to the west), the land was fertile, the climate clement and the area easily defensible.

After consulting with astrologers to confirm a judicious choice of location, al-Mansour set about employing the Arab world's finest architects to draw up plans and 100,000 masons and builders to complete them, pillaging stone from the ruins of Ctesiphon and Babylon to meet the demand.

The concentric design was born from the plan of a nomadic camp. This plan had previously been used in both Uruk and Hattra (two ancient Iraqi cities; the remains of Hattra in the north are breathtaking) and had significant strategic advantages. Two huge walls, 57m apart, were surrounded by a water-filled moat, with the space between them left empty for defensive purposes.

The whole structure was divided into four equal quarters by four roads, passing through a series of well-fortified and elaborate gates and sheltered by barrel-vaulted arcades. The roads led to the magnificent central complex, the Caliph's Palace, with its green dome topped by the figure of a horseman, spear in hand, marking the exact centre of the city. Next to the palace was the Grand Mosque, with both shielded from the rest of the city by a third protective wall. The space between the second and third walls was used to house the Caliph's prodigious retinue. The entire city had a diameter of approximately 2,700m.

Despite the garrison plan, al-Mansour named his new city Madinat al-Salaam,

Contexts

City of Peace, one of the names for paradise in the Koran. The four roads left for the four corners of the world, the gates through which they passed named after the nearest trading point: al-Kufa (southwest, a city near Najaf), al-Basra (southeast), al-Khorasan (northeast, a province in Iran) and Damascus (west). Baghdad quickly became a centre of trade for merchants coming from the Far East, the Mediterranean and surrounding countries, the circular plan of the city suggesting Baghdad's position as the vortex of the known world.

The relatively small confines of the city and its increased importance resulted in rapid extramural expansion. Bazaars and houses were set up around the outer wall, forming a district called al-Karkh (as it is known to this day) around al-Kufa Gate. On the other side of the Tigris, al-Mansour initially stationed a garrison before building a palace and mosque in 768.

The eastern bank was accessible via a pontoon bridge on the al-Khorasan road, and a similar explosion of markets and hotels grew up around the new palace, used by al-Mohadi, al-Mansour's son and heir apparent. The three main conurbations – Rusafa (still the name for the area around Baghdad Museum), al-Shammasiya and al-Mukharrim – formed the basis of the modern city of Baghdad.

By 946 the caliphate had abandoned the round-city and moved to the eastern bank and under Caliph al-Mustarshid-billah (1118–35) the semicircular eastern wall was constructed. While nothing remains of the old round city there are several reminders of the caliphate on the eastern banks of the Tigris, including part of the old wall and Wastani Gate (see pages 197–9).

History

EMPRESS IRENE'S TITHE

While still a young man, Harroun al-Rasheed was placed by his father, Caliph Al-Mohadi, at the head of an army of 95,000 to overthrow the Byzantines.

Harroun advanced to the Thracian Bosphorus. After defeating the Empress Irene's general Nicatas he marched to Chystopolis and conspicuously erected a camp on the hills opposite Constantinople. His intent was clear and Irene immediately dispatched ambassadors to sue for peace, but Harroun insisted that he would accept nothing but complete surrender. At this one ambassador supposedly told Harroun that the Empress had heard tell of his great military prowess and while he was her enemy, she admired him as a soldier. The flattery worked, and Harroun settled for an annual tithe of 70,000 pieces of gold.

The tithe was paid regularly for the rest of Irene's reign, the day on which it arrived was designated a holiday in Baghdad. The Roman soldiers would parade through the city with the gold before being graciously entertained and prepared for their return to Constantinople.

In 802 Nicephorus usurped the throne of the Eastern Roman Empire. In Edward Gibbon's account Nicephorus, 'resolved to obliterate this badge of servitude and disgrace. The epistle of the emperor to the caliph was pointed with an allusion to the game of chess, which had already spread from Persia to Greece. "The queen (he spoke of Irene) considered you as a rook, and herself as a pawn. That pusillanimous female submitted to pay a tribute, the double of which she ought to have exacted from the Barbarians. Restore therefore the fruits of your injustice, or abide the determination of the sword."' At this his ambassadors flung a bundle of swords at Harroun's feet. Harroun calmly drew his scimitar and smote the Roman swords in two with one blow, his blade remaining unscathed. 'In the name of the most merciful God, Harroun al-Rasheed, commander of the faithful, to Nicephorus the Roman dog: I have read your letter. You shall not hear my reply, you shall see it.'

Harroun immediately set forth for Constantinople ravaging Roman lands as he progressed. He laid siege to Heraclea (on the coast of the Black Sea), forced its surrender and sacked it. Nicephorus, realising the likelihood of defeat capitulated and agreed to continue paying the tithe, but no sooner had Harroun returned to Baghdad than Nicephorus again refused to pay.

Despite the treacherous winter conditions, Harroun immediately set forth for Phrygia in Asia Minor at the head of 15,000 men. In the ensuing battle the superior forces of Nicephorus were routed, he was wounded and 40,000 of his men killed. Nicephorus was forced to agree, once more, to pay the tithe.

But yet again the perfidious Nicephorus failed to keep his promise. Harroun vowed that the next time he set eyes on him it would be to slay him, but before Harroun could fulfil his vow he died.

History

The rise and fall of the caliphate

The economic flowering of Baghdad came during the reign of al-Mohadi and his successor, the fabled Harroun al-Rasheed (786–809). At the time of al-Rasheed Baghdad was the richest city in the world. Ships moored at its harbours bearing treasures from China, India, Sri Lanka and East Africa, the caliphate grew rich and spent liberally on the arts.

Although the Abbasids were Arabs, many had Persian blood flowing from their mother's side and they looked east for a model for their caliphate. By the time of the fourth caliph the Islamic ideal of equality had been lost in the heart of the round city. The caliph became known as 'The Shadow of God on Earth' and subjects were expected to fall down before him; gone were the days when Muslims only prostrated themselves before God. The pomp and ceremony, the fawning viziers, the slaves and the concubines are all immortalised in Scheherazade's tales of the *Thousand and One Nights*.

Al-Mahmoun (813–33) continued the caliphal patronage of scholars and artists. Founding the Bayt al-Hikmah ('The House of Wisdom'), he promoted the translation of ancient Greek and Latin texts on philosophy and science. Synthesising the knowledge and culture of India, Greece and Persia, Baghdadi scholars made huge advances in science, philosophy, astronomy, medicine, theology and the liberal arts. Poetry lost its dependence on classical form, becoming fluid, and writers began to write Arabic in prose.

But religious sectarianism and skirmishes with, amongst others, the Byzantines,

Contexts

had been weakening the caliphate from both within and without. As a result, al-Mu'tasim-billah (833–42) another son of al-Rasheed, was forced to relocate his capital to Samarra, about 100km north of Baghdad. By the end of al-Mu'tasim's reign the golden age of both the caliphate and Baghdad was over. Internal rebellion from imported Turkish bodyguards and an uprising of African slaves in the south of Iraq left the caliphate drained and anaemic.

Although Baghdad had retained its importance as a trading post, the return of Caliph al-Mu'tamid (870–92) to the city did little to revive its former splendour. Ensuing caliphs were forced to grant independence to more and more provinces and by the tenth century the Abbasid Empire consisted of little more than the modern boundaries of Iraq.

Denuded of their empire outside Iraq, the caliphate was then stripped of its power within. The introduction of the title 'Emir of Emirs' by Caliph al-Radhi-billah (934–40) fuelled internal unrest as local families fought for the honour. Finally claimed by a Shia tribe, the Buyids, they seized control of the caliphate's lands, leaving the caliph as little more than a figurehead.

During almost a century in power, the Buyids spread the faith of the formerly subjugated Shia and erected marvellous mausolea over the tombs of the Imams. Keen supporters of the arts during the time when rhyme came to poetry in Arabia, the Buyids failed to raise Baghdad to its former glory as Shiraz (Spain), Isfahan (Persia) and Cairo (Egypt) now wrestled for cultural pre-eminence.

In 1059 Baghdad changed hands once again when the Seljuk leader Toghril Beg

History

BAGHDAD IN THE THOUSAND AND ONE NIGHTS

There was in the time of the Caliph, the Prince of the Faithful, Harroun Al-Rasheed, in the city of Baghdad, a man called Sindbad the Porter. He was a man in poor circumstances, who bore burdens for hire upon his head. And it happened to him that he bore one day a heavy burden, and that day was excessively hot; so he was wearied by the load, and perspired profusely; the heat violently oppressing him. In this state he passed by the door of a merchant, the ground before which was swept and sprinkled, and there the air was temperate; and by the side of the door was a wide bench. The porter therefore put down his burden upon that bench. To rest himself, and to smell the air; and when he had done so, there came forth upon him, from the door, a pleasant gentle gale, and an exquisite odour, wherewith the porter was delighted. He seated himself upon the edge of the bench, and heard in that

wrested power from the Buyids and reinstated the caliph, who had been forced to flee the city. Although power remained firmly in the hands of the new conquerors the alliance was a happier one. The Seljuk Turks were Sunnis and together conqueror and caliph worked to eradicate Shi'ism from Iraq and the greater Seljuk Empire.

In the process some of the great Islamic colleges were founded in Baghdad, including the famous Nizamiya School, named after the vizier who founded it in place the melodious sound of stringed instruments, with the lute among them, and mirth-exciting voices, and varieties of distinct recitations. He heard also the voices of birds, warbling and praising Allah (whose name be exalted!) with diverse tones and with all dialects; consisting of turtledoves and hezars and blackbirds and nightingales and ringdoves and curlews; whereupon he wondered in his mind, and was moved with great delight. He then advanced to that door and found within the house a great garden, wherein he beheld pages and slaves and servants and other dependants. And such things as existed not elsewhere save in the abodes of Kings and Sultans; and after that, there blew upon him the odour of delicious exquisite viands, of all different kinds, and of delicious wine.

From 'The Story of Sindbad the Sailor and Sindbad the Porter' – adapted from 'The Arabian Nights', Lane's translation, OUP 1915, reprinted 1939.

1067, Nizum al-Mulk (see box, pages 198–8), and Mustansiriya School (see pages 192–4), built by the penultimate caliph, al-Mustansir (1226–42).

The Mongols

After ravaging much of Persia, Hulegu, grandson of Jengis Khan, issued Caliph al-Musta'sim, son of Mustansir, with an ultimatum to surrender. Hulegu had been encouraged by a Shia vizier named al-Alkami, who saw that this new conqueror could give him and his denomination power. Al-Musta'sim refused and in so doing sealed his fate as the last of the caliphs.

In February 1258 Hulegu took Baghdad. In accordance with his grandfather's precept to look kindly on those who capitulate and exterminate those who resisted, Hulegu mercilessly sacked Baghdad. An estimated 800,000 were slain. Buildings were razed, among them the House of Wisdom and its irreplaceable library, and the elaborate irrigation system dug up. The ashes of buildings mingled with the ink of thousands of books until, according to contemporary sources, the Tigris ran black. In the orgy of slaughter Hulegu showed mercy only to the Christian community, in recognition of his mother's and wife's religion.

Pushing west to further conquests, Hulegu placed al-Alkami in charge of the city. He ordered that religious buildings be reconstructed and put the former vizier in charge of restoring stability and prosperity. At Hulegu's death in 1265 his son Aba Qakhan, a Buddhist, took control of the city. At this time Buddhist temples were to be found dotted around Iraq, though none survived beyond the 14th century. Eighteen years later Takudar Il-Khan embraced the religion of his new subjects and set about restoring mosques and shrines including the Caliph's Mosque and the Souk al-Ghazil Minaret (see page 196).

The Il-Khan dynasty gave way to another Mongolian, Sheikh Hassan al-Jalayri. The Jalayrid dynasty met with some success, recapturing land and continuing to revivify Baghdad. Khan Mirjan, a vaulted caravanserai (see pages 146, 195–6) dates from this time, built by the governor of Baghdad, Amin-ed-din Mirjan, in 1357 as part of an endowment to the nearby school and mosque.

Then in 1392 the mighty Timurlane (a Mongolian conqueror, from Samerkand) descended on Iraq and sacked Baghdad, massacring its inhabitants. Despite a valiant and initially successful attempt by the Jalayrids to repulse him, Timurlane entered the city a second and third time. On the final attack Timurlane ordered his soldiers to kill everyone aged between eight and 80 and to pull down every building other than the mosques and hospitals. Furthermore, he also ordered each of the 90,000 soldiers to bring back a skull or face death himself. In *The Decline and Fall of the Roman Empire* Edward Gibbon notes:

> I have expatiated on the personal anecdotes which mark the character of the Mogul hero; but I shall briefly mention, that he erected on the ruins of Baghdad a pyramid of ninety thousand heads.

For the second time in 150 years, Baghdad and its population had been laid waste. There was no recovery from the ravages of this second assault and for the next hundred years Baghdad came under the rule of two Turkmen dynasties, the Black and the White Sheep. For a brief period subsequently, the Shia Safavid Persians controlled Baghdad, but in 1534 the Ottoman sultan Suleiman the Magnificent entered the city, ushering in nearly four hundred years of Ottoman rule.

The Ottomans

Although lengthy, much of the Ottoman rule in Baghdad was no less fraught than that of previous dynasties or empires. Constant skirmishes continued with the Persians and communication with the hub of the empire was at the mercy of volatile tribesmen. For much of the time, different parts of the country were semi-autonomous.

The conflict with the Persian Safavid Empire further entrenched the animosity between the Sunni and Shia. The Shia Safavids were the first to make Persia an officially Shia country, and with the holy shrines of Karbala and Najaf in Iraq, they remained eager to gain control of the entire country. The Ottomans, conversely, were desperate that the Shia faith should not spread beyond southern Iraq, using the northern half as a buffer with which to protect Turkey from Shia advance.

Both sides used religion as a rallying call among the people, for purely political ends, and both mercilessly subjugated those of the opposite sect.

Ottoman rule remained lax throughout the entire 400-year reign. The result was that power in Iraq slipped from the centre to a conglomeration of wayward tribal groups who fought for power amongst themselves, usually in narrow regions. By the end of Ottoman rule, these groups were both unused and unprepared to be governed by a central regime and there was little sense of nationhood.

Nevertheless, the long rule gave Baghdad a chance to recover. Living conditions were improved, hospitals and schools were founded and later factories were built. Control of the city was reorganised along more Western lines and toward the end of Ottoman rule, Baghdad became exposed to new European ideas.

Contexts

Further modernisation of the city took place under Madhat Pasha (1869–72) who set about introducing a new administrative system that included, among other advances, an elected town council. He opened the Baghdad-Kadhimiya tramway (no longer in existence), founded primary, secondary and military schools and introduced a press. The first newspaper in Baghdad, *al-Zawra*, rolled out in 1869.

World War I

Toward the end of the 18th century European powers were increasingly interested in the moribund Ottoman Empire. Eager to exploit the empire's natural resources, they also saw new markets for their products and were looking for a secure overland route to Eastern colonies. The provinces of Iraq were to play an important part in the ensuing political machinations.

By the turn of the century the British had oil interests in Iran and the south of Iraq and Baghdad was a vital communication link to India, with a large telegraph station in the city. It was still a transportation route, despite the opening of the Suez Canal, and there were fears that whoever ruled Iraq could pose a serious threat to British interests in the region, or even to India, the jewel in the imperial crown.

In 1902 Kaiser William II announced that a German company had won from the Ottomans the concession to build a Baghdad-Basra railway. Baghdad had been under the sway of British influence for some time and in the light of the Kaiser's policy of *Weltpolitik*, that sought to place Germany firmly on the world stage, and

History

THE PROCLAMATION OF BAGHDAD

'Since the days of Hulagu your city and your lands have been subject to the tyranny of strangers, your palaces have fallen into ruins, your gardens have sunk in desolation, and your forefathers and yourselves have groaned in bondage. Your sons have been carried off to wars not of your seeking, your wealth has been stripped from you by unjust men and squandered in distant places... it is [not] the wish of the British Government to impose upon you alien institutions.

'O people of Baghdad remember that for 26 generations you have suffered under strange tyrants who have ever endeavoured to set one Arab house against another in order that they might profit by your dissensions. This policy is abhorrent to Great Britain and her Allies, for there can be neither peace nor prosperity where there is enmity and misgovernment. Therefore I am commanded to invite you, through your nobles and elders and representatives, to participate in the management of your civil affairs in collaboration with the political representatives of Great Britain who accompany the British Army, so that you may be united with your kinsmen in North, East, South, and West in realising the aspirations of your race.'

Delivered by General Stanley Maude, March 1917

Contexts

the sensitive nature of the British involvement in Iraq, the move increased tension between the two countries.

In the approach to World War I the rate of construction on the railway increased and when war was declared in 1914 the Ottomans, hoping to gain protection against Russia, announced they were on the side of the Germans. Within months the British army invaded Iraq from the Persian Gulf. The army made rapid gains in the southern portion of the country but initial attempts to seize Baghdad were repulsed, resulting in surrender to the Turks at al-Kut, where the 9,000 men under General Townshend had been held under siege for 143 days.

With a change of command the British again advanced on Baghdad in December 1916, under General Stanley Maude. By March of the next year Baghdad had fallen. General Maude died in Baghdad of cholera later that year, but British interest in the region was still very much alive.

Three months after the British conquered Baghdad the Arab Revolt (a pan-Arab rebellion against Turkish rule) began under Sharif Hussein bin Ali, emir of Mecca, with the support of the British and French. His sons liberated swathes of Arab land from the Turks.

At the end of the war in the 1919 Paris Peace Conference, the League of Nations declared Iraq a mandate entrusted to Britain, while Syria was placed under French mandate. Later that year the French expelled Faisal, son of Sharif Hussein bin Ali, who had been declared king after liberating Syria from the Ottomans in 1918.

History

The British Mandate

Complete British control over Iraq was short-lived. The political problems that have always beset Iraqi soon flared up: conflict between Sunni and Shia, tribal leaders' insistence that their rights over land be confirmed, towns' demands that the power of tribes be curbed and the Kurds' desire for independence.

In addition, the Arab Movement had continued after the Arab Revolt and three powerful nationalist groups had formed: The League of the Islamic Awakening, The Muslim National League and The Guardians of Independence. For these groups the mandate was a betrayal of trust: they wanted an independent Iraq. In what was taken as a further slight, the British – eager to implement an effective administration swiftly – placed experienced Indian civil servants within the Iraqi administration.

In 1920 the country rebelled in the Great Iraqi Revolution. For three months the British tussled with various insurrections. The cost, around £40 million, was too high and the military regime was replaced by a provisional Arab government, aided by British advisers and watched over by the British high commissioner, Sir Percy Cox. Meanwhile, the British looked for someone suitable to take control of Iraq.

In Faisal, the deposed king of Syria, they found an ideal candidate. He was sufficiently sympathetic towards Britain, his role in the Arab Revolt would placate the nationalists, he was descended from the Prophet Mohammed and, although he was Sunni, the Hashimite family shared a grandfather of the Prophet with Ali, the first Shia Immam.

Contexts

Faisal accepted on condition that the choice was acceptable to his future subjects. The only problem was he was not Iraqi, but nonetheless a plebiscite returned a 96% approval. On August 23 1921, Faisal was crowned king of Iraq in the gardens of the Ottoman Palace in Baghdad (see pages 194–5).

The monarchy

Once a king was installed upon the throne, the British set up an indigenous army, but demanded that Faisal sign a treaty with Britain to protect her interests. The conditions were almost the same as those of the mandate: to respect religious freedom, to respect foreigners, to treat all states as equal and to co-operate with the League of Nations.

At the same time Britain was to advise on matters of state involving domestic and foreign affairs including finance, the military and the judiciary. Unsurprisingly, the nationalists were not happy.

Meanwhile in Britain, there was an election to win and the national press had launched a popular campaign against the cost of involvement in Iraq. Navigating between the British electorate and the Iraqi nationalists, the treaty was finally ratified in 1924, but only after its duration was dropped from 20 to four years and Britain threatened to refer the matter of non-co-operation to the League of Nations.

Once the treaty had been signed a constitution was put in place. It called for a constitutional monarchy, a parliamentary government and two chambers, namely, an appointed Senate and an elected House of Representatives. The latter was to be

History

elected every four years, but the details of the Organic Law, as it came to be known, left the balance of power firmly with the monarch.

The new constitution brought little stability – in just over 30 years, the prime minister was changed an astonishing 45 times – and the old problems of governance, tribal power, ethnic division and religious sectarianism dogged the new government. But added to them was a new division: pan-Arabism versus Iraqi Nationalism.

Although political parties were quick to form, many ran on single-issue agendas, usually campaigning for independence from the British. The dual rule, from both without (the hand of Britain) and within (the newly appointed government), became known as 'the perplexing predicament', perhaps theoretically possible, but untenable in practice.

In 1932, Iraq officially joined the League of Nations as a fully independent state. The parties who had based their manifestos on independence melted away, their *raison d'etre* gone.

Independence

For a brief period after independence it looked as though internal divisions might be dropped in the pursuit of internal reform, but this was short lived. In 1933 the Assyrians, a northern group of Christians who were fearful of suppression, demanded an increased assurance of their rights and an autonomous state.

King Faisal was out of the country and the party in power, keen to impress the public with its strength, called in the army and brutally crushed the uprising. On his return to Baghdad, Faisal found deep and irreconcilable fissures in the political system. Before he could even attempt to remedy the situation, he died.

The politically endorsed suppression of the Assyrians was a watershed, marking the entrance of the military into Iraqi politics.

When the British first established an indigenous military it rapidly became the most organised and efficient element in the new system, primarily because military structures were an already familiar concept. Owing to this, the power of the military strengthened as the newly imposed and alien political order increasingly struggled to find its feet.

Additionally, it had been expedient to place Sunni soldiers (who had served under the Ottomans) in the commanding positions and fill the ranks with Shia tribesmen. This set-up crystallised, perpetuating the traditional Sunni supremacy over the Shia within the most powerful organ in the country.

Educated in the West, Faisal's 21-year-old son, Ghazi, had little idea how the tribal system worked and could not command the loyalty that his father had utilised. With a young and inexperienced king, the political system span into further decay.

Governments were constantly beset by attempts to oust them, with three main tactics being employed by rival factions: press campaigns highlighting personal and political intrigues; inciting tribes in areas hostile to the current government; and soliciting support from the army.

In 1936 the Middle East's first military *coup d'etat* saw Hikmat Sulaiman instated as prime minister and the Shia General Bakr Siqi as chief of general staff. For a brief period the coup thrust the Sunnis and pan-Arabism out of the political limelight.

Once politics had been militarised it was impossible to turn back to civilian rule. Until the army's defeat in 1941 at the hands of the British the tide of short-lived prime ministers was turned by military factions.

To compound matters Ghazi was killed in a motorcar accident in 1939, conspiracy theorists claim at the hands of the British. His four-year-old son, Faisal II, ascended to the throne under the regency of his uncle Abd al-Ilah.

Pan-Arabism continued to grow in strength and with it a hatred of Britain. Despite Nuri al-Said's – a long-standing advisor of the monarchy and nine-time prime minister of Iraq – attempts to align Iraq with the Allies, the government of the time refused under the pretext that British victory was not then assured. Extremists of the pan-Arab movement tried to persuade the government to throw in their lot with the Germans as the most likely to promote independence and unity among the Arabs. In 1940, secret negotiations with the Axis powers began.

This alliance came to an abrupt halt when British reinforcements arrived in 1941 and the pan-Arab leader and his supporters fled the country. Iraq officially declared war on the Axis powers in 1942 and Britain gained use of transportation and communications facilities within the country.

But nationalist sentiment had been stirred up and after the war the continued pro-British leaning of Nuri al-Said did little to engender stability. Political activity, prohibited during the war years, was restarted in 1946 although several of the leftist parties were considered too extreme and Nuri al-Said had them closed down.

Increasingly the old guard were coming into direct collision with a new generation of politicians and politics.

The Iraqis had been among the founding members of the Arab League in 1945, and had also joined the UN later in that year. When the UN decision of 1947 to partition Palestine was announced, unrest bubbled in Baghdad and 10,000 Iraqi soldiers were sent to participate in the Arab-Israeli War of 1948.

Poorly equipped after cutbacks in military spending post-1941 (when the British temporarily suppressed the military) they fared badly and returned further alienated from the pro-Western monarchy. The 1948 war had also set the country back economically as 40% of available funds went to the army and Palestinian refugees, while at the same time the lucrative oil-line to Haifa was severed and Iraq's oil revenues were halved.

To compound matters a Jewish businessman was lynched, prompting a mass exodus of the rich Jewish community. Between 1948 and 1952 around 120,000 Iraqi Jews were airlifted to a new life in Israel in Operation Ezra and Nehemiah.

Popular nationalist sentiment came to a head with the 1948 uprising (*wathbah*). Already roused by the Palestine issue, a severe bread shortage and strong anti-government sentiment, a relatively mild joint defence agreement with Britain known as the Portsmouth Treaty was the final straw. Street uprisings and riots lead to violent clashes between students and the police and the treaty was revoked.

The situation did not settle. In 1952 another major uprising occurred, fuelled by economic depression (exacerbated by a failed harvest) and a lack of political freedom. The mob turned violent in Baghdad, the police were unable to cope and the army was called in. Martial law was imposed on the city for two months, the return to civilian rule saw few changes and, driven further underground, political parties became increasingly radical.

At around the same time, Iraq's oil revenues quadrupled and expensive showcase developments were begun. The nominally apolitical Development Board set about constructing ambitious flood prevention schemes, irrigation systems, bridges, schools, a new parliament and a new palace. But these were long-term projects and the people saw little immediate benefit.

At the same time, increasing national revenues from the oil boom had promoted inflation, squeezing the poor. Paltry salaries, increasingly out of kilter with their qualifications, disillusioned the burgeoning middle classes whose ranks were swelled by education drives that enabled the upward movement of some among the working class.

Externally the government had made a series of foreign-policy blunders. Syria rejected advances for a political union with Iraq. The British-supported Baghdad Pact, a treaty of mutual defence between Iraq, Turkey, Iran and Pakistan, threatened Egypt and President Gamal Abdul Nasser launched a stinging press campaign calling for the Iraqi army to overthrow the regime. Finally, when King Hussein of Jordan and Faisal II formed a joint Hashimite kingdom (the Arab Union) to counterbalance the unification of Egypt and Syria, the monarchy divorced itself completely from popular opinion.

The country was ripe for revolution.

Revolution and the Republic

While the young politicians tried to dent the political bulwark of the older generation, young soldiers, unable to become directly involved in politics, began to think of revolution. Under Brigadier Abdul Karim Kassim, anonymous cells of 'Free Officers' plotted the overthrow of the monarchy, guided by a group of 14 officers called the Central Organisation. When the brigades in which Kassim and his close associate Abd al-Salaam Arif were ordered to the Jordanian border in case of Israeli attack, the plan became clear. During the march north they would pass through Baghdad.

On July 14 1958, the 19th Brigade stormed the royal palace in a swift and bloody pre-dawn coup. Almost the entire royal family and their entourage were executed, including al-Said, captured as he tried to escape dressed as a woman. Kassim became president and commander of the national forces, appointing Arif minister of the interior and deputy commander.

Once in power the group proved to be built on shifting ideological sand that rendered it almost immediately unstable. Kassim believed in Iraqi nationalism, Arif favoured pan-Arabism and advocated union with the United Arab Republic (a union of Syria and Egypt) and the revolution had once again stirred up the perennial religious and ethnic rifts.

Kassim prevailed and, increasing his links with the nationalist Iraqi Communist Party (ICP), he set about improving conditions for workers. In the process he passed Public Law 80 that denied foreign companies concession rights to oil and significantly increased the government's income.

History

FRANK LLOYD WRIGHT

In 1952, after the negotiation of a 50-50 deal with the British Petroleum Company began to fill the imperial coffers, King Faisal II launched a series of ambitious architectural projects. Designs were commissioned from Le Corbusier (who continues to be a source of inspiration in Baghdad; his plans were later incorporated into Shahaab stadium near the police academy), Walter Gropius (Baghdad University) and in 1957, Frank Lloyd Wright.

Initially commissioned to design an opera house for a small plot of land in downtown Baghdad, it is said that while flying over the city he noticed Edena Island in the middle of the Tigris and asked to use that instead. The King supposedly replied 'The Island, Mr Wright, is yours!'

The opera house is one of Wright's most ambitious projects, the car park alone, based on a three-tier ziggurat design, was to provide space for 1700

But there were many, especially supporters of Arif and pan-Arabism, who were disillusioned with the revolution. The ICP seemed to be getting out of hand and communist demonstrations had turned to massacres in both Kirkuk and Mosul. In 1959 the newly formed Baath Party carried out an assassination attempt against Kassim. The young party member who tried to kill him was Saddam Hussein.

Despite surviving the attempt on his life, unrest amongst the Kurds and his vehicles. In the centre of the car park was to be the many arched and highly ornate opera house, decorated with characters from the *Thousand and One Nights* and surmounted by a dome shaped like a Saracen helmet.

In addition to the opera house, Wright designed an art gallery, a museum, a postal-telegraph building and a monument to Harroun Al-Rasheed, the latter based on the Melwiya at Samarra.

Unfortunately the revolution of 1958 swept away the possibility of funding designs dismissed as 'rather grandiose'. Frank Lloyd Wright died a year later, but not before designing the Grady Gammage Memorial Auditorium at Arizona State University in which echoes of the failed Baghdad Opera House can be seen.

Frank Lloyd Wright's designs for Baghdad can be viewed at www.geocities.com/SoHo/1469/flw_iraq.html.

controversial foreign policy sealed Kassim's fate. He deliberately provoked Iran by claiming additional land in the Shatt al-Arab and claimed Kuwait as the 19th governerate of Iraq (both causes which Saddam Hussein would later take up). Fellow Arab countries and the West denounced the latter, which would have left Kassim isolated but for his continued relationship with the Soviet Union.

In February 1963, Kassim was successfully overthrown by the Baath Party.

History

Coups and counter coups

Once in power the tiny Baath ('Rebirth') Party, numbering fewer than 1,000 members, set up the National Council of the Revolutionary Command. Its leader, Ali Salih al-Saadi appointed Arif as president and Ahmed Hassan al-Bakr, a former Free Officer from Tikrit, prime minister.

The ideology of the Baath Party was too vague to solve the problems that beset Iraq and win it popular appeal and as a result opposition was rabidly suppressed. Furthermore, without a strong ideological basis with which to win supporters, recruits were increasingly drawn from the same tribe or town as important figures, a practice that accelerated in the 1970s and led to the dominance of the al-Tikritis.

Within the year Arif, with the aid of military leaders and the Nasserites (supporters of Nasser and pan-Arabism), had ousted the fledgling Baath Party.

With his hands now firmly on the reigns, Arif set about preparing Iraq for integration with Egypt (the union with Syria had failed in 1961) that was expected to occur in 1966. In the process he instigated Nasser's socialist reforms and nationalised all essential industry and infrastructure.

In 1965 the proposed union fell through, prompting an unsuccessful Nasserite coup against Arif. Less than a year later, in April 1966, he was killed in a helicopter accident.

For the next two years the tension between pan-Arabism and nationalism continued, accompanied by renewed ethnic conflicts. A civilian government tried unsuccessfully to push through reforms. The failure of Iraq to support its Arab brothers in the six-day war against Israel of 1967 caused massive popular unrest and

Contexts

the government, propped up by an assortment of self-seeking military officers, was again primed to fall.

The Baath Party takes control

After its overthrow in 1963 the Baath Party was further beset by a bitter ideological struggle between Marxist and Nationalist factions that ended only with the election of a strong leader, the former prime minister Ahmed Hassan al-Bakr, a year later.

Bakr, a Sunni from Tikrit, began to form around himself a cadre of officials bound to him by blood or tribal duty, not simply by ideology. By the time the Baath Party came to power in 1968, Tikritis dominated the political scene. Also of critical importance, in light of the military lobby directing Iraqi politics, the majority of key Baath figures were already drawn from the armed forces.

The Baath Party had also gained support and expanded after setting up regional branches. But perhaps the most important change was brought about during a reorganisation in 1967, which established a party militia and an intelligence branch.

On July 17 1968, an uprising lead by Bakr with the support of three senior military commanders (Col Abd al-Rahman al-Daud, Col Hammad Shihab and Col Abd al-Razzaq al-Nayif) overturned the government, replacing it with the Revolutionary Command Council (RCC). The RCC immediately assumed supreme authority over Iraq with Bakr as president and al-Nayif as prime minister.

Within days, on July 30, a group of ambitious Baath supporters led by Saddam

History

Hussein removed the officers al-Nayif and al-Daud from power. The Baath Party were truly in power.

The highly organised Baath Party immediately began to infiltrate almost all national organisations, thereby both consolidating its power base and ensuring that dissidents could be more easily monitored.

An attempted coup led by Nasserites and conservative members of the military was not only crushed but also provided an excuse to purge the country of dissent. From 1968 to 1973, a series of sham trials leading to execution, assassination and intimidation effectively cleansed Iraq of any immediate challenge to Baath rule.

There was still a threat from within. A failed revolt led by the head of the secret service, Nazim Kazzar, in 1973 saw the intelligence service both purged and restructured to limit its power. Increasingly, intelligence became a web of grass-root networks spread across the country.

Further precautions were taken to bolster the party: in 1974 the Regional Command (the party's highest executive body) was officially given sole power to make new policy; by 1977 the Regional Command was populated only by members of the RCC; and in 1978 an expanded militia was formed, numbering around 50,000 men.

Meanwhile a series of personal tragedies and illness suffered by Bakr meant that from the mid-70s power was increasingly devolved to his deputy. In July 1979 Bakr resigned and Saddam Hussein succeeded him as president of the Republic.

Build up to the Iran-Iraq war

Throughout the 70s relations with Iran became increasingly fraught. In 1971 Iran claimed that Iraq had failed to abide by the 1937 border treaty and re-opened the dispute over the Shatt al-Arab. When Iraq refused to negotiate the Shah sent Iranian ships through Iraqi territory without paying the required dues.

In response Iraq began to aid anti-Shah revolutionaries, causing the Shah to retaliate by funding and arming Kurdish dissidents.

This was particularly important given increased Kurdish unrest that was threatening to destabilise Baathist sway over Iraq. To settle the Kurdish problem the Baath initially negotiated a deal with Mustafa Barzani (father of the Governing Council member), head of the Kurdish Democratic Party (KDP). This lead to a modicum of peace until 1974.

In 1974 fighting again broke out between the military and the Kurdish Pesh Merga (Barzani's troops) after a failed attempt by the Baath Party to assassinate Barzani and his sons. When the Baath signed a deal with the Soviets, stopping what had been a vital source of support for the Kurds, it looked as though the government had won.

Instead the Kurds turned once again to the Shah for support. With heavy artillery from Iran and some additional help from Syria, Israel and the USA, the Kurds inflicted significant damage on the Iraqi army.

Fearing a drawn-out crisis Saddam started negotiations with the Shah. On March 6 1975, Iraq agreed to Iran's border demands and the Shah agreed to stop funding the Kurds and to tighten border security to prevent supporters crossing into Iraq.

History

Cornered and without help the Pesh Merga (literally 'Those who Face Death') were soon defeated.

In 1979 the Shah was deposed and the Shia-cleric Ayatollah Khomeini gained power. Shia-Sunni relations in Iraq were already delicate and the Sunni-driven Baath Party feared that the new Iranian government would feed the political aspirations of the restive Shia population.

There was also personal animosity between Khomeini and Saddam Hussein, the latter having exiled Khomeini from Iraq in 1977 where he had lived (in Najaf) for 15 years. At the same time, Iran was weakened by the internal turmoil. This presented Iraq with the perfect opportunity to consolidate its position as a leading Arab state and regain the disputed territory that had been lost in 1975.

The short fuse was finally lit in 1980 by an assassination attempt on foreign minister Tariq Aziz perpetrated by an Iranian-funded organisation, the Shia al-Dowah al-Islamiyah (lead by Ayatollah Muhammad Baqir al-Sadr).

In retaliation Saddam Hussein hanged both al-Sadr and his sister and executed 97 members of the al-Dowah. He also declared the return of lands lost to Iran in 1975. Iran failed to comply, Ayatollah Khomeini declared that the Iraqi Baath Party wanted to ignite a war against Islam, and on September 23 1980, Iraq invaded Iran.

The Iran-Iraq War

The eight-year Iran-Iraq war (1980–88) can be divided into five main phases; Iraqi advances, Iraqi retreats, the war of attrition, the war of cities and the tanker war.

Contexts

Oil revenues of US$21.3 billion assured Saddam that his country could easily afford to go to war. Moreover, intelligence sources gave good reason for optimism. His Arab army numbering 190,000 men was well armed with the latest Soviet technology and could boast 2,200 tanks and 450 aircraft.

Furthermore, the fabled Persian army was in a shambles after the upheaval of the Revolution. Iraqi command also believed that after the fall of the Western-friendly Shah, Iran would have increasing difficulty obtaining spare parts for its US manufactured armoury. The air force, stocked with the latest US planes, was the only immediate cause for concern, prompting Iraq to launch a massive pre-emptive attack on Iranian airbases.

Strengthened hangers and massive airfields meant the strike was not hugely effective and within hours Iranian F-4s had attacked strategic sites around Iraq's main cities.

Baghdad had expected the minority Arab population of Iran to rise up in support, but despite the failure of this to materialise, Iraqi forces on the ground had more success than the initial aerial assaults. The element of surprise enabled six army divisions to press on into Iranian territory and capture several strategic sites, regaining the Shatt al-Arab in the process. With 1000km² of Iranian territory captured, Iraq offered a peace settlement. Iran refused.

Instead the Iranian air force was strengthened by the release of experienced pilots gaoled during the Revolution, and the ranks of the army were swelled by volunteers, many of whom were fighting for an ideology and believed that

History

martyrdom on the battlefield would ensure them entry into paradise. Some went into battle with the keys of heaven hanging round their necks.

The 'human wave' offensives of the Iranian forces had some success and Iraq, hampered by a sensitivity to casualties, failed to initiate new attacks against recaptured sites. In the first three years of the war 60,000 Iraqis are believed to have lost their lives. The Iranian toll was twice as great and the number of wounded, many times higher.

In spite of heavy losses and Saddam's withdrawal of troops to the internationally recognised border, Iran once again refused a settlement deal in 1982.

By 1984 the Iraqi strategy had shifted from attack to defence, and increasingly military tactics were employed to force Tehran to negotiate a deal. Iraq purchased expensive new weapons, primarily from the Soviet Union and France, constructed the 'killing zones' (artificially flooded areas of land around Basra) and targeted Iranian shipping, thereby creating further economic havoc.

As the Iraqi death toll continued to rise inexorably, the army began to use chemical weapons (on at least 40 occasions between 1981 and 1984) to wipe out or debilitate the enemy from a distance. The UN finally condemned the atrocities in 1986, citing the use of nerve and mustard gas and berating Iraq for contravening the 1925 Geneva protocol on chemical weapons.

In 1984, lacking equipment to deal with Iraqi minefields and quagmires, the Iranians once again turned to 'human wave' tactics. Journalists at the time reported seeing groups of 20 children or more roped together dragging potential defectors into battle.

The year 1985 saw a new phase in the war in which major cities and industrial complexes were increasingly the target of attack on both sides. Iran also began to spot-check shipping in the Persian Gulf, hoping to disrupt supplies headed for Iraq.

Both sides increased attacks on oil tankers suspected of dealing with the opposition, though many were neutral ships belonging to neighbouring countries. Between them 111 neutral ships were attacked in 1986 alone, including an Iraqi missile attack on USS Stark and an Iranian attack on a tanker flying the US flag (of Kuwaiti origin, it had been re-flagged after Kuwait asked for protection).

Both the direct provocation and the West's dependence on oil supplies from the region led to increased international interest. By 1988 the Persian Gulf was being patrolled by no fewer than 18 international navies, with ten flying Western flags.

UN Resolution 598, seeking to halt the war, was passed unanimously on July 20 1987. Iran initially rejected it on the grounds that Iraq was not sufficiently punished for initiating the war.

After the intense 'War of the Cities' in 1988, which saw 190 missiles rain down on Iranian cities in the space of six weeks, Tehran began to rethink its position. Thirty percent of the residents of Tehran had fled and a renewed use of chemical weapons by Iraq in the south left the threat of long-range use on a major conurbation hanging in the minds of the Iranian leadership.

In August 1988, Iran accepted the terms of Resolution 598, a ceasefire was called and the war was finally over. Almost nothing had been achieved save economic and human disaster for both countries. The leaders who began the conflict ended the war still in control of their countries, and the disputed Shatt al-Arab borders remained much as they had been in 1980.

The human cost was staggering, estimated at up to a million and a half dead, with many more wounded and up to one million displaced. The estimate of the number of Iraqis killed in battle as a percentage of the total population is equivalent to around 5.6 million in a population the size of the USA.

The financial cost was equally debilitating. Iran spent US\$74–91 billion plus a further US\$11.26 billion on military imports. The Iraqi equivalents totalled a phenomenal US\$94–112 billion and US\$102 billion on military imports.

Many prisoners of war on both sides were never told that the war had ended. It is believed that some may still be languishing in prison, despite an official exchange of POWs in 1998, ten years after the war ceased.

The Anfal

During the Iran-Iraq war, Baghdad had largely ignored the increasing power of the Kurds in northern Iraq, primarily because internal strife would have drained resources from the primary conflict.

In the final stages of the war Kurdish rebels flexed their new might when they joined Iranian troops in a northern offensive, threatening Iraqi oil fields around Kirkuk. Saddam handed over emergency power to Ali Hassan al-Majid (Chemical Ali as he later came to be known), giving him almost presidential sway over Kurdistan.

Rural villages were singled out for harbouring Pesh Merga or their sympathisers and became prohibited zones. Under military directive SF/4008 of 1987, army commanders were ordered to

> Carry out random bombardments, using artillery, helicopters and aircraft, at all times of the day or night, in order to kill the largest number of persons present in these prohibited zones...All persons captured in those villages shall be detained and interrogated by the security services and those between the ages of 15 and 70 shall be executed after any useful information has been obtained from them, of which we should be duly notified.

The horror of Halabja, the Kurdish border town in which up to 5,000 civilian residents were killed in a Sarin gas attack in 1988 is well known, but this was not an isolated incident (and was not strictly speaking part of the Anfal). On April 15 1987, Iraq earned the gruesome distinction of being the first government ever to use chemical weapons against its own population, when aircraft dropped poison gas on the Patriotic Union of Kurdistan (PUK) and KDP headquarters.

Chemical attacks on villages swiftly followed. After the first wave of civilian attacks, victims were dragged from hospital beds in Irbil, where they had sought treatment for severe blistering, burns and blindness. None was ever seen again. In the following 18 months over 40 chemical attacks were documented.

The Anfal (or 'Spoils', the eighth *sura* of the Koran) proper began in February 1988, as an eight-stage process aimed at purging Kurdistan of all rebel factions. Far

History

from being a clandestine attrition, the successes of each stage were glorified by the Iraqi media, directed from Baghdad.

The stages demarked geographic areas and in each the same method was employed: aerial chemical bombardment using a lethal cocktail of mustard and nerve gases, a military attack on fortified positions, razing, looting and destruction of all human habitation by ground troops and finally a demolition crew sent in to flatten entire villages. Rings of trucks surrounded villages waiting to transport the population to holding centres, while patrols hunted down anyone who tried to escape into the countryside.

The Anfal officially ended in April 1989. The campaign had left at least 50,000 civilians (some estimates claim double that number) either missing or dead and half of Iraq's arable land destroyed. The Kurds hope that Saddam Hussein will be fully held to account for his involvement when he comes to trial.

The invasion of Kuwait

Two years after the end of the Iran-Iraq war, Iraq was once again dragged into conflict. In mid-1990 Saddam accused Kuwait of depressing oil prices and initiating 'economic warfare' against Iraq. Talks failed and Baghdad additionally accused Kuwait of stealing oil from its Rumaylah oilfield.

On August 2, Iraq attacked Kuwait in a lightning operation. The Emir fled and Iraq rapidly secured the entire country, claiming it as the 19th governorate. In a further act of provocation the Iraqi army massed along the border with Saudi Arabia.

The world was quick to respond to this flagrant violation of the sovereign rights of a pro-Western ally. Sanctions were imposed within days and Iraqi oil exports halted. The UN Security Council convened and Resolution 678 was passed in November, allowing 'all necessary means' for the restoration of peace and security to the region. The UN gave Saddam Hussein until January 15 1991 to remove all troops.

Meanwhile at the request of the king, US forces gathered in Saudi Arabia and France and Britain announced that they would send 10,000 troops to the Gulf. By January over half a million allied troops were deployed in the region, but the sabre-rattling failed to initiate a withdrawal and after the collapse of several high-level diplomatic initiatives Baghdad decided to go to war.

A coalition of 28 UN members (including non-combatants such as Afghanistan, Honduras and Bangladesh) launched the first Tomahawk missiles simultaneously from the Persian Gulf and Red Sea on January 17 1991. The devastating offensive consisted of air campaigns as well as the use of naval forces.

The allied campaign sought to knock out Iraq's infrastructure and demoralise the army (although the attack on Amiriya air-raid shelter in Baghdad, in which 400 civilians were killed is testimony to the inaccuracy of some targeting – the shelter is now a museum). In total 109,876 Coalition sorties were flown and the US air force alone dropped 60,000 tonnes of bombs.

In return Iraq launched a SCUD missile attack against Israel, hoping to provoke Israel into joining the war as a combatant, thereby potentially splitting the Arab

History

THE FIRST FITNA: THE ORIGINS OF THE SUNNI-SHIA SCHISM

At his death in AD632 the Prophet Mohammed left no intimation of whom he would like to guide the new Muslim community. It was decided among the leaders of the group that a khalifa (caliph) be appointed, but there was some dispute over who should take on this role. Abu Bakr and Umar ibn Al-Khattab, two of the closest companions of the Prophet, were the most influential members of the community, but some thought that the title should go to a member of the Prophet's family. The most obvious choice was the young and pious Ali ibn Abi Talib, the Prophet's cousin, ward and later son-in-law. This suggestion was dismissed due to Ali's age and lack of experience and Abu Bakr was elected as the first caliph. Umar (634–44) became the second Caliph and it was under his rule that the Arabs defeated the Persian army at Quadisiya (Ctesiphon, just outside Baghdad). The Arab empire expanded under Umar, but in 644 he was killed in Medina by a Persian prisoner of war. Six of the prophet's companions elected Uthman ibn Affan, another of the Prophet's son-in-laws, to succeed him as the third caliph. Despite the continued success of the Arab empire Uthman's detractors, mainly the Muslims from Medina, loathed his habit of giving out the best government positions to his Umayyad relatives and dissent brewed. It finally came to a head in 656 when Uthman was assassinated by a group of soldiers who pronounced Ali caliph.

Despite Ali's popularity in Medina and among nomadic tribes, especially those in Iraq, the assassination of Uthman caused rupture within the hitherto peaceful Muslim community. Although Ali had not condoned the murder, the repercussions lead to five years of civil war, known as the first fitna.

Among the many battles that Ali was forced to fight was the Battle of The Camel, so called because Aisha, the beloved wife of the Prophet, observed the proceedings from the back of a camel. Ali's forces won this battle, waged after Ali failed to meet the demands of Aisha and a companion of the Prophet that he punish those who had killed Uthman. Attacked from the north by the new Umayyad caliph, Muawiyya, and from within by a new group the Kharajis (they disliked Ali's partial submission to Muawiyya and that he had never avenged Uthman's death and reverted to what they saw as the pure, egalitarian origins of Islam) Ali was forced to retreat to his capital in Kufa. In 661 Ali was murdered by a Kharajite in Najaf.

After his death, Ali's son Hassan came to power. Almost immediately he came to an agreement with Muawiyya, renounced any involvements in politics and retired to Medina until his death in 669.

continued overleaf

THE FIRST FITNA
continued from overleaf

When Muawiyya died the group based in Kufa who had remained loyal to Ali called on his second son, Hussein, to rule over them, rather than Muawiyya's son Yazid I. Hussein set forth from Mecca with some loyal aids and their families. While still on their journey, Hussein heard that the Kufans had withdrawn their support after being threatened by the local Umayyad governor. He pressed on, none-the-less, believing that the sight of the Prophet's grandson and his family on the march would convince the Kufans to change their minds. Instead, on the plain around Karbala Hussein's group was surrounded by the Umayyad army and massacred. Hussein was the last to die, holding his baby son in his arms as he fell. The death of Hussein further united the group who called themselves Shia-i-Ali (the Party of Ali) against the Umayyad caliphate. Every year the Shia remember the death of Hussein on the day of Ashura; under Saddam the traditional festival in Karbala was banned.

The Shia revere Ali, Hassan and Hussein as the first three of 12 Imams, all descended from Ali and the Prophet's daughter Fatima.

Contexts

members of the alliance. Israel was narrowly dissuaded from retaliating after promises of protection from the USA.

At the end of January, Saddam gave the order to set light to Kuwaiti oilfields and start pumping crude oil into the Persian Gulf, leading to large-scale environmental damage. By mid-February the oil slick contained an estimated 1.5 million barrels of oil.

When the ground war was finally launched on February 24, the Iraqi forces in Kuwait were already beaten. The air strikes had severed supply and communication lines and many soldiers simply laid down their arms. Where the Allies encountered resistance, usually from élite forces such as the Republican Guard, superior weaponry and training guaranteed victory.

On February 26, just three days after the ground war commenced the announcement came from Baghdad that Iraqi troops would leave Kuwait. The allies took Kuwait City, and on February 27, President George Bush *père* announced a ceasefire to enable the remaining Iraqi troops to leave Kuwait.

On March 3, Iraq officially accepted the ceasefire and the international war was over.

The end of the war saw large-scale uprisings among the Shia populations of the south and the Kurds in the north, after having been encouraged to 'take matters into their own hands' by George Bush. These were brutally crushed after the allies withdrew. In Hilla alone (100km south of Baghdad) 3,000 Shia were slaughtered, felled by machine-gun fire as they stood in the pits that were to become their graves. Many of these mass graves were unearthed in May 2003.

In the north the Kurds fled into the mountains. With Kurdish refugees dying at

THE SECOND SALADIN

Saladin, or Salah al-Din Yusuf Ibn Ayyub, was born in the town of Tikrit in either 1137 or 1138. Of a prominent Kurdish family, the young Saladin initially showed little military prowess, being more interested in the study of religion than of warfare. Under his uncle Shirkuh he helped to topple the Shia Fatamid Empire based in Cairo and on the death of Nur-al-din, he proclaimed himself Sultan of Egypt in 1174. Once in control he set about establishing Cairo as a centre of orthodox Sunni Islam, founding religious schools, importing preeminent teachers from the East and building mosques. In the West Saladin is best known for vanquishing the crusader forces at Hattin (near Tiberius) in 1187 and capturing Jerusalem from the Christians. Thousands of Christian prisoners were subsequently marched to Cairo to work on extending the city's fortifications. This precipitated the Third Crusade of 1189 and the celebrated meeting of Saladin and Richard I (Coeur de Lion) of England, the subject of many chivalric tales. The result of the Third Crusade was the signing of the Peace of Ramala that granted the Crusaders a strip of land

the rate of 450–750 per day due to diarrhoea, acute respiratory infections and trauma, Britain, France and the USA imposed an air exclusion zone over the north and south of the country.

Contexts

along the coast from Tyre to Yafo, Saladin remaining in control of Jerusalem.

Approximately 800 years later, in the town of Tikrit, Saddam Hussein was born on April 28, 1937.

Playing on this coincidence (some say he deliberately moved the year of his birth) Saddam increasingly sought to portray the similarity between himself and the greatest Arab conqueror. In 1998 stamps were issued with Saladin placed slightly behind Saddam implying a direct succession, the Dome of the Rock in Jerusalem placed in the background. Murals, particularly in Tikrit, reinforced the connexion. Emulating his hero, both savant and strategist, Saddam wrote novels (three in total), poems and played the lute. A widely circulated children's book tells tales of Saladin's bravery in the face of the infidel before swiftly moving on to the story of the second Saladin, Saddam. But the symbolism was more than an infatuation with a hero; Saladin had regained Jerusalem for the Arabs, and sent the infidel into bondage. Saladin was a potent symbol of Saddam's ambition to forge in Iraq a new centre of Arab military strength, to regain the Holy Land and to vanquish the 'Great Satan'.

In Operation Provide Comfort a safe haven for the Kurds was declared in the north, which resulted in virtual autonomy and de-facto independence. A Kurdish army patrolled the border and in 1992 free elections were held.

History

AN IRAQI ARTIST
Esam Pasha, Baghdadi Artist

Under the previous regime I faced two difficulties; I was Iraqi and an artist. As an artist I wanted to paint the emotions that I felt, but as an Iraqi I always had to worry about which paintings I dared take out of my studio and which of my sketches I should hide and never paint. The latter were usually drawn when thoughts of freedom carried me away as I worked; the end results were too contentious to show to anyone but a few trusted friends – when showing such drawings one mistake could be the final one. Saddam's regime used to kill or torture people for creating ambiguous works, on the off chance that they be interpreted as anti-establishment. This almost happened to me when I took a painting depicting a falling eagle to an exhibition; fortunately a friend at the State Art Centre saw it and said in a low voice, 'Take it away quickly before anybody else sees it and thinks you mean the regime is falling.'

I have never painted anything for Saddam and now I am proud to be painting the first post-war mural over one of his huge portraits. Now artists can express themselves without fear. Under Saddam there was one rule: everything is denied unless it is obligatory.

Sanctions

The sanctions imposed by the UN in August 1990 were never lifted after the war. Prohibiting the import (except for medical supplies) and export of any goods not directly permitted by the Security Council, they were described by the State Department as 'the toughest, most comprehensive sanctions in history'.

The results were devastating. Infant mortality soared (to one of the highest in the world according to a UN report), malnourishment, particularly among children, became endemic with 25% of those under five being classified as chronically malnourished. Simple diseases became deadly, the infrastructure crumbled and prices soared. A WFP report estimated that by 1995 average shop prices had rocketed to roughly 850 times what they had been in 1990. As prices soared, salaries plummeted to an average professional salary of US$3 per month, down from US$200 in 1985. Many were forced to sell everything they possessed simply to survive. As a last resort many sold themselves or committed suicide.

In April 1995 the UN passed Resolution 986 which lead to the instigation of the 'Oil-for-food' programme in December 1996. The programme allowed Iraq to export up to US$2 billion of oil every six months (the cap was removed in 1999 under UN Resolution 1284), and from the revenues generated to import essential goods, subject to approval by the UN Sanctions Committee.

The oil-for-food programme was only ever intended to be a temporary measure and in 2001 the Secretary General of the UN wrote, 'the programme was never meant to meet all the needs of the Iraqi people and cannot be a substitute for normal economic activity in Iraq.'

Although changes were made to the initial strictures and there were some signs that malnourishment figures had improved, Iraq was still groaning in poverty. A professional's monthly salary could buy two chickens or a lipstick and many people had to sell the food they were given in order to buy clothes and shoes.

While the population was in penury, loopholes and the black market enabled Saddam to commence building the two largest mosques in the world, enormous structures in the heart of Baghdad (one is almost complete). Construction was a way around the sanctions for the rich – certain buildings were deemed permissible by the UN and excessive material requirements were submitted at inflated prices. As a result, such buildings blossomed around Baghdad.

Throughout sanctions the rich became richer. Doctors in Baghdad, recounting the time under sanctions, describe how patients died for want of medicines that had been on the list of Iraqi imports. Expensive Western drugs, they were secretly re-sold abroad to bankroll the excesses of the regime. When Saddam Hussein celebrated his 64th birthday in 2001, the party cost an estimated US$8 million.

Weapons of Mass Destruction

Under the ceasefire agreements of 1991, Iraq was obliged to destroy all nuclear-, biological- and chemical-weapons capabilities as well as all delivery systems with a range greater than 150km.

Contexts

During inspections in the mid-90s, inspectors found considerable supplies of biological weapons, long-range missiles and a clandestine nuclear programme. Despite such successes the inspectors were constantly hampered by the regime and both the United Nationals Special Committee (Unscom) and the International Atomic Energy Agency (IAEA) were forced to leave Baghdad in December 1998, during the US-UK Operation Desert Fox, aimed at intimidating Saddam into compliance. They had neither completely verified Iraqi disarmament, nor put into place the ongoing monitoring system necessary to ensure Saddam did not continue or restart any prohibited programmes.

In addition to sticks, various carrots were extended to persuade Saddam to comply with inspections. A provision in UN Resolution 1284 said that sanctions would be lifted if the Iraqi government was found to have complied fully with the United Nations Monitoring, Verification and Inspections Commission (Unmovic, formerly Unscom) and the IAEA for a period of 120 days. Both agencies would then have the power to re-impose them with five days' notice if any further breaches occurred.

Between 1998 when Unscom left and 2002 when Unmovic and the IAEA were readmitted, no external record was available of the state of WMD production in Iraq. Meanwhile the devastating attacks of September 11 2001 had changed the world's outlook on terrorism and rogue states.

On September 24 2002, the British dossier on Iraq's alleged WMDs (the September Dossier) was released, followed two months later by UN Resolution

1441. Unanimously passed, Resolution 1441 accused Iraq of being in 'material breach' of its commitment to disarm and demanded that Iraq immediately co-operate fully both with Unmovic and IAEA. Both organisations were to be given complete and unimpeded access to anything that they wished to inspect or analyse. This included immediate access to any of Saddam's eight palaces. Furthermore they were entitled to interview anyone without state observers.

Iraq was given seven days to notify the UN that it was willing to comply and 30 days to compile a complete inventory of all aspects of its WMD programmes. Inspections were to begin within 45 days and a report was to be delivered to the Security Council within 60 days or sooner if Iraq failed to comply.

On December 7, Iraq delivered an 11,807-page overview that purported to be the complete inventory required by the UN. This proved to be little more than a re-hash of previous lists. When Hans Blix, chief weapons-inspector, gave his brief to the Security Council on March 7, although remaining non-committal, he listed at least 100 unanswered questions.

The Security Council was split. The US and UK put forward a further resolution, authorising the use of force if Iraq was found not to have complied with Resolution 1441. Russia, China, France and Germany vehemently disagreed.

With no obvious chance of reconciling differences the US declared its resolve to act unilaterally on March 18, and weapons inspectors were pulled out of Iraq. Bombing began two days later and on March 21 the Coalition army captured Umm Qasr, Iraq's only deepwater port. Operation Iraqi Freedom had begun.

Timeline of Operation Iraqi Freedom
March

19–20	US and UK forces invade Iraq actively supported by Australia, Spain and Rumania
21	Umm Qasr, Iraq's only deepwater port, captured
22	US tanks push on to Baghdad, Iraq ignites trenches of oil to obscure the capital. UK and US forces meet resistance around Basra
23	US-led forces move to within 160km of Baghdad, but meet severe resistance around Nasiriya and Najaf
24	US-led forces, now only 115km from Baghdad, are impeded by fierce sandstorms. US troops land in the Kurdish controlled north
25	President Bush asks Congress for US$75 billion to pay for the war
26	Now within 100km of the capital, Iraqi forces attack vital Coalition supply lines, tailing over 300km
27	Around 1,000 US paratroopers land in Kurdistan
28	Kurdish forces claim to be within 25km of Kirkuk as they press into Saddam-controlled Iraq
29	Humanitarian aid arrives at Umm Qasr on the *Sir Galahad*. A suicide car-bomb kills four US soldiers; Iraq announces that this is to become a military tactic
31	The Republican Guard show signs of weakening in their defence of Baghdad

History

April

2   Minister of Information Mohammed Saeed al-Sahaf tells the Iraqi people that Saddam calls for a holy war against the Coalition invasion

4   US Army 3rd Infantry Division captures Baghdad International Airport

5   US-led troops enter Baghdad from the south, but do not cross the river; they meet with severe resistance

6   Thousands of Baghdadis flee the city as US-led troops again enter Baghdad and US warplanes continue their 24-hour aerial patrols overhead

7   British troops consolidate control of Basra

8   US-led forces fan out across Baghdad. Two journalists are killed when the US targets their hotel

9   US-led forces take control of Baghdad, toppling a huge statue of Saddam in Firdos Square. The devastating looting continues; some claim to have received encouragement from US troops screaming 'Take your piece of Saddam's oil.' Hospitals plead for military assistance that fails to materialise and many are completely gutted. Iraq's only secure mental asylum, in Baghdad, is destroyed by looters when a tank punctures its outer wall after mistaking it for a prison. Highly dangerous patients escape – all records are destroyed in fires

10   Kirkuk is taken, the Iraqi army offering no resistance. In Baghdad the looting continues largely unhindered by Coalition forces

11   Coalition seeks support of clerics to contain the frenzied looting and distributes lists of the '55 most wanted'. Mosul falls to Kurdish forces

Contexts

12	Looting continues and Iraq Museum loses priceless treasures
13	Iraqi policemen are recalled to their jobs in an attempt to restore order
15	Tikrit falls and the US declares the end of major fighting in Iraq; troops begin to withdraw
17	The UN lifts sanctions on Iraq
21	Thousands of Shia pilgrims go to Karbala for a formerly banned celebration

May

| 1 | Bush declares the war officially over, standing before a banner proclaiming 'Mission Accomplished' |

IRAQ TODAY

After the fall of Baghdad (April 9 2003), Saddam's Republican Palace became the base for Coalition operations and the first interim administration, the US Office of Reconstruction and Humanitarian Assistance (ORHA). A large area around the palace, including the Conference Centre and al-Rasheed hotel, was closed off and became a heavily fortified area known as the Green Zone.

By the end of the first month of occupation the security and political situations had shown no signs of improvement and the operation was re-branded as the Coalition Provisional Authority (CPA). Equipped with more power and more money, an administrator, L Paul Bremer III, was placed in charge.

In May the Baath Party was officially dissolved and a process of 'debaathification'

Iraq today

began, to remove senior Baath Party members from governmental positions. Party membership had facilitated promotion and as a result many institutions were forced to place inexperienced staff in key positions or to invite ex-patriot Iraqis to return; the latter has remained controversial among the population at large. This problem continues to face the new government.

The Interim Governing Council met for the first time in July 2003. Many of its members were returning exiles accused of being out of touch with Iraqi needs and, having been appointed by the CPA, it faced an up-hill battle to prove that it was more than an American puppet. Although under the ultimate authority of Paul Bremer, the IGC had several key powers, including the right to choose UN representatives, select the current cabinet and, crucially, produce an interim constitution.

The interim constitution was finally signed on March 8, after severe internal differences threatened to derail the attempt to find a code acceptable to all. The major rift occurred between the majority Shia Arabs and the minority Sunni Kurds.

The Shia representatives wanted a constitution containing no more than general principles, leaving a democratically elected government (in which they expect to be the majority) to fill in the details. The Kurds, anxious that they will loose their voice in a united Iraq after over a decade of independence (Turkey has made it clear that it will not tolerate an independent Kurdistan), insisted that a clause be inserted giving them the power to veto any future constitution. This was eventually agreed.

Under the constitution, Iraq becomes a democratic, republican, pluralistic state.

The official religion is Islam, which will be a source of law, but not the primary source. The aim is for a quarter of the national assembly (which will be elected in 2005) to consist of women – a target few Western democracies can boast.

The last few months of CPA control were marred by increased violence, more casualties, and allegations of the torture and systematic abuse of prisoners in Abu Ghraib, once Saddam's infamous political prison. Militias loyal to the young Shia cleric, Moqtada al-Sadr, took on coalition forces in the southern half of the country and hundreds were killed in a month-long offensive against the mainly Sunni city of Falluja, in a bloody attempt by US forces to flush out terrorists.

The insurgents increasingly aimed their larger attacks at 'soft' Iraqi targets. Over 100 Shia pilgrims were killed during the festival of Ashura, and hundreds more Iraqis have been killed in bombs around the country, mainly directed at the new Iraqi Police Force and Iraqi Army. Iraqis seen as working for the coalition (however obliquely) received death threats, forcing many to stay at home.

Meanwhile, the foreign community faced a new threat: kidnap. Most of those captured were released, but after several beheadings, many of the few remaining NGOs left, along with some contracting firms. The remaining foreigners in and around Baghdad massively cut back on operations and bunkered down.

As violence escalated in the approach to June 30, the date set for the official hand-over, the coalition secretly brought forward the ceremony in a move designed to undermine any coordinated attack. On Monday June 28, at 10.17 local time, Paul Bremer transferred sovereignty to the interim government and left Iraq.

The interim government is headed by Shia prime minister, Iyad Allawi, supported by a mainly ceremonial president, Ghazi Mashal Ajil al-Yawir, a Sunni.

The timetable to full sovereignty should see elections to a national assembly in January 2005, a referendum to endorse a new constitution in autumn 2005 and full elections for a new government in December 2005, with the government taking power in January 2006. Coalition forces remain in Iraq for the foreseeable future.

ECONOMY

The economy of Iraq has been shattered by three wars, over 12 years of debilitating sanctions and a greedy élite who siphoned funds from the people to pay for opulent lifestyles.

Iraq's foreign debt currently stands at an estimated US$130 billion, much of it a hangover from the Iran-Iraq war. Some countries have indicated that they may be willing to write off or significantly reduce obligations.

The World Bank estimates that reconstruction will cost an estimated US$56 billion. The US has pledged US$20 billion and at the Madrid donors' conference in October 2003, a further US$13 billion was promised. Many donor countries were later aggrieved when the Coalition announced that non-participant countries would be initially excluded from bidding for primary contracts.

With the August bombing of the UN headquarters (which killed, among many others, the UN Special Envoy Sergio Vieira de Mello) and later the bombing of the

Red Cross headquarters, both withdrew from Baghdad. Many other NGOs followed suit, further slowing the recovery of both Iraq and its capital.

Iraq has suffered not only years of financial crisis, but also an intellectual one. Once boasting the largest number of PhDs per head of any country, a brain drain, erratic schooling during sanctions (when poorer children stayed at home to work) and plummeting professional salaries has left the country in intellectual turmoil.

Emigrants have failed to return in large numbers due to the continued unrest and lack of security and the large percentage of the population formerly employed by the army has had to seek jobs elsewhere.

Compounding the unemployment issue (currently estimated at 45%) is an increasingly Anglophone business world: large foreign contractors require their employees to speak English. Although many Iraqis have the skills required, very few who have not studied English as a major at university (and are therefore usually unqualified to rebuild infrastructure) speak the language to a workable level.

Some large international businesses have arrived, but the physical danger in setting up offices has deterred many well-known brands, and most are taking a 'wait and see' approach.

Under Saddam Hussein the economic functioning was based around a command economy, with a few elements of a free-market, usually riddled with nepotism and cronyism. Under sanctions, Iraq was allowed to export oil only in return for restricted imports.

Economy

With the overthrow of the former regime, the Coalition is intent on turning Iraq into a fully functioning free-market economy. For the first time in decades foreign nationals are allowed to set up business in Iraq and to hold shares in Iraqi companies, although there is a question mark over what laws will be repealed once an elected government is in power. Baghdad stock exchange is open for business once again.

Iraq's wealth relies on vast oil reserves, but through disrepair and attack it now lacks the capability to produce at anywhere near capacity. Shortly after the war production was down to a meagre 700,000 barrels per day. If current facilities are restored Iraq is believed to be capable of producing 2.8–3.0 million barrels per day. When achieved, export revenues would be between US$19–25 billion and with further investment are believed capable of reaching US$50–60 billion within ten years.

Although 40% of the workforce is thought to be employed in agriculture, the years of mismanagement of arable land has led to a significant fall in production primarily due to increased salinisation. Some land is now unworkable as a result.

Manufacturing remains a small sector with tobacco, leather goods, construction materials and processed foods being the most commonly produced.

RELIGION

Representing 96% of the population, Islam is by far the dominant religion in Iraq, but within this religious group there is a split between the majority Shia (about 60%) and the minority Sunni (about 35%) Muslims. In addition, between 4–5% of the population belong to minority religious groups, mainly Christian.

Contexts

While representing only a tiny fraction of the religious make-up of the country, several religions have strongholds in Iraq, in particular the Yazidi (erroneously called 'devil-worshippers'; they practise a religion with a strong Gnostic influence and were brutally persecuted under Saddam) and the Mandaeans (a Nestorian group who follow John the Baptist) who have an important branch in Baghdad. The once large and prosperous Baghdadi Jewish community is now reduced to approximately 23 individuals.

Religion is of huge importance in Iraq. In many ways the history of the country is the history of its religion. The great Shia-Sunni schism (the first in Islam) occurred in Iraq and the rift festers to this day (see pages 42–4).

Much of the increased tension in post-war Baghdad is fractured along religious lines and recent reports have indicated terrorist organisations may be hoping to capitalise on religious sensitivity.

PEOPLE

The population of Iraq is believed to be 24,680,000 (CIA Factbook estimate July 2003), growing at an estimated 2.78%. In 1932 the population of Baghdad was still a tiny fraction of today's crowded city at a mere 358,840 inhabitants. Since then the population has exploded, current estimates placing the population around 5.6 million, though the precise figure remains speculative.

There are two major ethnic groups in Iraq, the Arabs and the Kurds, the latter found mainly in the northern regions. In addition there are minority groups of

Turkmen, Assyrians, Armenians and Yazidi. Recent estimates split the country as follows: Shia Arab 60%, Sunni Arab 18%, Kurdish 18% (the Kurds are also Sunni) and Other 4–5%. Within each of these splits are found different tribal groupings.

In 2000 approximately 90,000 Palestinian refugees were living in Iraq.

An estimated 3.5 million Iraqis live abroad. Mass emigration has particularly decreased the percentage of Christians (usually of Assyrian or Armenian ethnicity).

Look out for the blue eyes of Baghdad; they are surprisingly common and invariably bewitching.

SYRIAC

Syriac, the language spoken at home by the Assyrian Christian community in Iraq, is derived from the branch of Aramaic that Jesus would have spoken. Aramaic played an important role in early Christianity; many scholars believe that Mark's Gospel was originally written in Aramaic and only later translated into Greek.

With the rise of Edessa, a small, independent, Christian state in what is now southeast Turkey, the importance of the Edessene dialect (that spoken today) increased and it became one of the major literary languages of Christianity. Its flexibility and lack of rigid syntax made it ideal for transmitting complex theological thought. The influence of Syriac and Christianity spread along the

CLIMATE AND GEOGRAPHY

Iraq, a country of varied geography, is a little larger than Sweden or California. In the north is a mountainous region and in the southeast, bordering the Persian Gulf, the delta region of the rivers Tigris and Euphrates creates a large swathe of marshland. Most of the marshes were drained by Saddam Hussein, but projects are now in place to re-flood sections. To the west of the Euphrates desert rolls out to Syria, Saudi Arabia and Jordan, claiming 35% of the country. Between the two rivers is a fertile alluvial plain, in which Baghdad is located.

With the world's second-largest reserves, oil is the chief natural resource, but

silk routes, bi-lingual tablets in Chinese and Syriac dating from AD781 have been found in Xi'an in Western China and the written form of Jengis Khan's Mongolian dialect was based on Syriac script.

Although the majority of modern Iraqi Assyrians come from the north, there is a large community in Baghdad. Saddam Hussein forbade the use of Syriac in churches, but churches in the city (both Syrian Orthodox and Chaldean Catholic) now, once again, conduct weekly services in Syriac and visitors are warmly welcomed.

Words in English of Syriac origin include, abbey, abbot, damson, Mammon and muslin (which means literally 'linen from Mosul').

there are smaller deposits of coal, salt, sulphur and gypsum.

The climate in Baghdad is extremely variable dependent on the time of year. A law passed under the former regime proclaimed a public holiday whenever the temperature reached 50°C or above. Iraqis joke that from early July until the end of August the official thermometer remained stuck on 49°C.

In reality, temperatures regularly enter the high-40s in the shade, and with zero cloud cover throughout the summer there is no respite from the searing sun. Even in the relative cool of the evening, temperatures seldom sink below 30°C. These extreme temperatures, coupled with humidity as low as 10% in the afternoon, can be fatal and any indication of heat-stroke or heat exhaustion should be taken seriously.

The summer months are also plagued by *shamal*, a hot, dry wind from the northwest that often brings with it blinding sandstorms.

By the end of September the cool weather has set in, and the autumn is exceptionally pleasant. Days of warm sunshine are punctuated by the occasional day of cloud and rain, giving welcome variety after the monotonous skies of summer.

The winters in Baghdad are surprisingly cold, with temperatures scraping 0°C at night, and the wet weather can make the city less appealing. The increase in humidity brings misty mornings, which combine with the pall of pollution hanging over the city to produce a beige smog. Although it is rare for temperatures to dip below freezing during the day, an extreme of −7.8°C has been recorded in January.

Spring is once again a balmy season, with warm sunshine and showers although the risk of sandstorms begins to increase.

Contexts

FLORA AND FAUNA

The once-rich wildlife of Iraq has suffered from chronic over-hunting; the last lion was shot in 1910, wild asses, oryxes and ostriches are on the verge of extinction and otters no longer sport in the southern marshes. Wildcats, jackals, hyenas and gerbils are now the most common wild mammals.

In more settled times gazelle are hunted (usually from 4WD) and the Christian community enjoys shooting and eating the wild boar found in remoter regions. For those interested in reptiles there is an endangered species of tortoise to be found in the desert.

Choruses of wild dogs may keep you awake at night and sinuous cats sneak in to steal food, but in common with most capital cities, there is little genuine wildlife in Baghdad. At night the occasional bat can be seen swooping around, and if you are exceptionally lucky and live in a leafy area you may chance upon a hedgehog, long-legged and less rotund than its European counterpart, a toad or a scuttling, brown lizard. Hedgehogs are captured for their use in arcane magical charms and toads are valued for their medicinal properties. At Baghdad racetrack toads are regularly used to cure bone-splits; the toad is split in two and bound around the affected limb for 24 hours, reducing swelling and softening bony growths.

Unless you make a trip to the bird market, where a flamboyant selection of finches and parrots are for sale, you will probably never see anything more exciting than a pigeon or a crow and even these are not common. Migratory birds are caught in their thousands every year in the wintering grounds of southern Iraq; many end up in Baghdad's market, many more in the pot.

As you drive out of Baghdad you may be lucky enough to see the soaring silhouette of an eagle, a kite or a vulture and along the pampas grasses lining the rivers the occasional heron or stork.

Cockroaches, ants and spiders are not a particular problem, but in the hot summer months mosquitoes storm the city.

An aerial view of Baghdad is surprisingly green and the banks of the Tigris were once 'black with trees' as an Iraqi put it, a reference to the verdant parks that lined the river where families would stroll and eat fish. An increasingly paranoid Saddam Hussein denuded much of this area, fearing that unseen attacks could be launched against his palace complex, a defensive tactic continued around the city by the Coalition in 2003. The palace complex itself is now called the Green Zone, a reference to the heavily planted grounds.

Apart from the grasses and reeds lining the banks of the Tigris the green of Baghdad comes mainly from date palms and huge eucalyptus trees, their branches dipping and cascading as though rebelling against the ramrod back of the palm. Fruit trees, in particular the pomegranate and orange, are found in gardens with flowering, pink oleander. Do not be tempted to pick the flowers of the oleander, a plant whose beauty belies its toxicity.

Contexts

Planning

2

A PRACTICAL OVERVIEW

Baghdad is a sprawling city of 5.6 million people divided into two halves by the River Tigris (Dijla in Iraqi). River traffic is almost unseen, but the many bridges that cross it form vital arteries: Baghdad is very much a split city and the river is often crossed and re-crossed many times in a day. Closure of any major bridge leads to traffic mayhem.

Although blocks of flats are scattered around the town, there are few genuine high-rises and those there are are mainly hotels and ministries. Baghdad has crept outward from the river, covering a considerable area, and is yet to explore a third dimension. Additionally, there is no obvious centre. As a result transport and the expectation of hours wasted in traffic are essential for anyone needing to move around the city.

The street system in Baghdad is based on numbered streets off a few main streets or squares that are named. The names have changed frequently and few streets are well marked. To compound matters, Saddam Hussein banned maps and guidebooks of Baghdad in the 1980s.

As a result a curious phenomenon of Baghdad is that few people actually know the address of where they work or even live, and everyone navigates using landmarks and main streets. It was easier to find somewhere described as 'opposite the carpet-shop, with a blue gate, in X', than follow street and sector numbers without a map. Baghdad policy is that if you get lost, just ask, and in a city in which nobody's business is their own someone will always be able to point you in the right direction once close enough. It is yet another reason, however, why it is unwise to attempt to go anywhere without someone who knows the city and can speak fluent Arabic.

Baghdad is generally a friendly place and whoever you are you will probably fit into a niche with relative ease. Finding like-minded people will never be hard – the flip side is that you will find there are an equal number ready to contest your lovingly held opinions, and often vociferously.

WHEN TO VISIT

For the few who have the ability to choose when to visit Baghdad, the autumn and spring are the best times to see the city. From late September, the temperature is pleasantly hot, edging toward cool by the end of November. The deep-blue sky, one of the most memorable features of the city, is broken up by spattered cloud cover and the sunsets are probably some of the best you will ever see. December and January can be quite chilly and wet. Certainly avoid travelling to Baghdad in the summer months when the heat is unbearable, even to the local population.

Be aware of the dates of religious festivals if your trip is short or urgent: government offices are closed and translators more expensive. In particular note the dates of Ramadan. Baghdad as a city is far more liberal than many Middle Eastern capitals (although this may change), but you may feel uncomfortable eating, drinking or smoking during the day during Ramadan – especially if those you are with are fasting – and you should always be discreet. Many restaurants close during the day and a large number have shortened evening hours and limited menus. Alcohol can still be bought from street-sellers, large hotels and some restaurants, but is less freely available. The Shia and Sunni celebrate the end of Ramadan at slightly different times, resulting in a week's holiday during Eid al-Fitr.

HIGHLIGHTS

The Iraq Museum, with its once astonishing Sumerian and Assyrian collections, should be a highlight of any trip to Baghdad. Unfortunately, after the much-publicised looting, the museum is closed until 2005 at the earliest while an intensive cataloguing is undergone to assess the true extent of the damage. In addition structural improvements are due to be made.

Other highlights include Mustansiriya School, the oldest Islamic college in the world, and the Shia shrine at Kadhimiya, especially if you don't have time to visit either Karbala or Najaf.

On the outskirts of Baghdad, Ctesiphon, a Parthian ruin with one of the largest freestanding brick arches in the world, and Agargouf, the remains of a ziggurat, are certainly worth half a day. If you have time only to make one full day trip, don't miss Samarra; the Melwiya is a breathtaking and unique monument, and the view from the top is stunning. Be aware, however, that Samarra is in the restive Sunni triangle.

Finally, no trip to Baghdad is complete without a boat trip down the Tigris, if the situation permits.

THE NUMBER SEVEN

In shops and houses around Baghdad you will often see the *sabaa aiyun*, or 'seven eyes' ornament. Made of bright blue ceramic, the most common is a hexagon pierced by seven holes, believed to bring blessing on the building.

The number seven is important in Islam (as well as in Christianity and Judaism), but its significance stretches back to the Sumarians. In the Epic of Gilgamesh, set somewhere between 2750–2500BC and recounting the adventures of the King of Uruk (perhaps the origin of the name Iraq), the number 14 is repeatedly replaced by the stronger seven and seven.

'Tammuz, the lover of your earliest youth...You loved the supremely mighty lion, yet you dug for him seven and again seven pits. You loved the stallion... yet you... ordained for him to gallop for seven and seven hours'

Later, Babylonian ziggurats were composed of seven tiers, attributed to the 'seven heavenly bodies' of their astrological system and Babylonian harps were strung with seven strings, one for each note of their scale.

July, the seventh month, is Tammuz in Arabic, named after the Sumarian god of agriculture (later worshipped as the sun-god by the Babylonians). Before the national Iraqi census of 1957, and the introduction of identification cards, no birth records had been kept. Anyone born prior to 1957 was given the same birthday – the auspicious, 1st of Tammuz.

PUBLIC HOLIDAYS

Iraq is such a mixture of different religions and cultures that holidays can crop up at unexpected times. Under the former regime employees were allowed to take days off to celebrate their religious festivals, and in the current political vacuum this is still the accepted norm. Many of the old official holidays were either related to the Baath Party or Saddam Hussein and have of course disappeared, but they may well be replaced with others in the future. At the moment the following still stand:

Jan 1	New Year
Jan 6	Day of Establishing the Iraqi Army
March 21	Festival of Spring, Nawrooz
April 9	Day of Saddam Hussein's downfall (probable holiday)
May 1	Labour Day
July 14	Day of Establishing the Republic of Iraq
August 8	Peace Day

Friday is an official day off, and Thursday is a half-day.

Major Islamic religious holidays

The Islamic calendar is based on lunar months and as a result the dates of Islamic holidays move within the Western year. All dates can vary with the sighting of the moon.

Public holidays

	2004	2005	2006
Eid al-Adha (Festival of Sacrifice)		Jan 21	Jan 10
Muharram (Islamic New Year)		Feb 10	Jan 31
Ashura		Feb 19	Feb 9
Mawlid al-Nabi (Prophet's Birthday)		Apr 21	Apr 11
Start of Ramadan	Oct 16	Oct 5	Sep 24
Eid al-Fitr (Ramadan ends)	Nov 14	Nov 4	Oct 24

TOURIST INFORMATION

There is relatively little tourist information available on Baghdad. Saddam Hussein banned the publication of guidebooks when he banned maps about 20 years ago. Once you arrive, copies of the old Ministry of Culture guidebook to Iraq are for sale in hotels (although you'll probably need to understand another European language to read one as the English edition has all but sold out) along with some equally antiquated maps.

Some of the websites listed at the back will give overviews of the country and a historical perspective. Whatever the reason for your visit you should do some thorough research on the current situation, and these websites may help.

The Department of Tourism (in the Ministry of Culture) is housed in the old fashion house on Palestine Street, near al-Rubayee Street. The staff are friendly and helpful, but their job isn't really to show tourists around. A proper tourist office is yet to be set up.

Some tourist agencies near the Sheraton and along Saadoun Street are opening up, but as yet are so underused that specific recommendations would be inappropriate.

Planning

Realistically, once you hire a translator/driver (see *Private car*, page 114, and *Translators/drivers*, page 187) you won't really need anything else: they'll know the city well and will almost certainly be more than willing to check places out in advance or find you additional information (usually in Arabic).

Until the security situation returns to normal avoid being part of a large group of Westerners when travelling around the city.

INTERNATIONAL TOUR OPERATORS

At least two international tour operators plan to visit Iraq in 2004. Hinterland Travel has plans for a tour from Europe to Syria and Iraq. LIVE Travel have conducted several successful trips to Iraq and intended to run more in 2004; however, they have decided to suspend them for the time being. Check their website for updates.

Hinterland Travel Geoff Hann, 12 The Enterdent, Godstone, Surry RH9 8EG; tel: 01883 743584; fax: 01883 743584; email: hinterland@tinyworld.co.uk

LIVE Travel Phil Haines, 120 Hounslow Road, Twickenham TW2 7HB; tel: 020 8894 6104; fax: 0870 138 6931; email: phil.haines@live-travel.com; web: www.live-travel.com

TIME DIFFERENCE

Iraq is at GMT +3, but normally operates daylight saving time from April 1 until October 1, when the clocks go forward by one hour to GMT +4.

Note when travelling in and out of Iraq that the neighbouring countries all have their own time rules: Syria is always 1 hour behind Iraq. In Jordan standard time is

GMT +2, but they operate on permanent daylight saving of GMT +3. Iran is GMT +31/2 and GMT +41/2 from March 21st to September 23rd. Kuwait and Saudi Arabia are on standard time GMT +3 and do not operate daylight saving. Turkey conforms to EU time rules (ie: in changing its clocks on the same days each year), and is GMT +2 in winter and GMT +3 in summer.

RED TAPE

Visas are now required, although the process is very much in its infancy. At the time of writing visas take between ten and 15 working days in most countries as the application form must be sent to Iraq for processing. The embassy in Jordan can process visas in 1–3 working days (Sat–Thu morning). Visas cost US$30–50. Two passport photographs and a completed application form (available from Iraqi embassies) are required. For the time being anyone in possession of a CAC, old CPA or new US Embassy badge may enter Iraq without a visa.

There is no ban on entry with Israeli stamps and holders of Israeli passports have been known to enter without a problem. It remains to be seen whether the new Iraqi government will decide to re-impose the ban. They may also see fit to reinstate the compulsory AIDS test.

Iraqi embassies

Iraqi Embassies are currently established in only a few countries. For an up-to-date list including contact numbers, go to http://www.iraqmofa.net/english/dim/iraqm.aspx

Amman Between 1st & 2nd Circles : tel: +962 6 4623175/6/7/8;fax: +962 6 4619177/4637328
Madrid Tel: +91 3885980/7591282; fax: +91 7593180
Moscow: tel: +007 095 2465506/2465507; fax:+007 095 2302922
Paris 53 rue de la Faisanderie - 75016 Paris; tel: +33 145533370; fax: +33 145533380
Rome Tel: +39 06 2210672; fax: +39 06 2233902
Washington 1801 P St NW, Washington DC 20036; tel: +1 212 7374433; fax: +1 212 7374434

GETTING THERE AND AWAY

Baghdad lies at a crossroads and theoretically there are many ways to reach the city. By far the most popular starting point is Amman from where you can choose between the painfully long road journey and the painfully expensive flight.

At the time of writing (July 2004), the Amman–Baghdad highway is subject to a high number of attacks, both from bandits and terrorists and should be avoided. There are efforts in place to secure this primary route into Baghdad, so check the current situation. The owner of the al-Saraya hotel (email: saraya-hotel@index.com.jo)) will be able to provide sensible advice, if necessary. The safest way to enter Baghdad is by air from Amman, although the road from the airport to the centre of town is considered one of the most dangerous in the world. If the cost of flying is too high, the roads into Baghdad from the South are currently more stable. Consider travelling from Kuwait or Basra while the Amman–Baghdad highway remains volatile.

Via Jordan

By road, the 660km journey takes around 11 hours at a conservative estimate, longer on the return. Shortly after the war convoys of GMCs (large four-wheel drives) would travel together for safety, leaving Amman at around midnight and staying at the border until first light when the mad dash for Baghdad would be made. Many foreigners still choose to travel in convoys and if you are in a non-taxi GMC this is certainly advisable. The road is still dangerous and attacks by armed bandits occur, particularly near the flash-point town of Fallujah.

From **Baghdad to the border** the highway is wide and well made, apart from one off-road diversion due to a bombed bridge. Unused and faintly surreal picnic tables still line the road at intervals, and the endlessly flat expanse of rocky desert stretches out to shimmering horizons. It is beautiful at dawn, when the sun rises over the flat plane, but can be dazzling and unrelenting during the day, punctuated only by the occasional bombed bridge and numerous burnt-out cars.

Several service stations provide food, WCs and petrol at reasonable intervals, but be cautious when using them as foreigners have been shot in wayside shops.

At the Iraqi border hand over your passport to be stamped. A brief search may also be made. Once at the Jordanian border the queuing begins in earnest; waits of seven hours are not unknown, but expect to be held for at least two. The earlier you arrive the shorter the queue.

Cars are emptied and every item of baggage scanned and searched. Make sure you keep a close eye on all your luggage. Before entering into Jordan you must buy a two-week visa from the visa office. This costs JD10 and must be paid for in Jordanian dinar; a bureau de change is nearby.

Large or expensive items must be signed for as 'personal use only' and may be marked in your passport (one journalist is now bearing a passport which lists 'One computer with hard drive, one preserved dog', after taking a stuffed wolf through customs). All papers for vehicles, including a fully up-to-date *carnet de passage* must be in order and presented in full. Don't worry though, your driver will shepherd you through the system, and shared taxis will always wait.

The Jordanian border has a duty free, cafeteria and small shops. Despite the singularly unpleasant nature of the lavatories you will probably be grateful for them by the time you get there. There are no amenities at the Iraqi border.

Once in Jordan the road narrows to a bumpy and undulating single carriageway for the rest of the journey. The landscape, however, is fascinating, having changed to a deep rust-brown desert covered in spherical black boulders.

When going to **Baghdad from Amman**, the border crossing is relatively swift. Passports must be handed into the passport control office, where you wait among swarms of people until your name is read out. The exit visa costs JD5, unless you are on a 24hr transit through the country, when there is no payment.

If your company has not provided transport then the easiest way to find a GMC to Baghdad from Amman is to leave a message on the media noticeboard in the Hotel Intercontinental. Alternatively, the friendly owner of the al-Saraya Hotel (a good place to stay if you can't afford five-star, the al-Saraya has become a legendary

BAGHDAD–BASRA
Rosie Garthwaite

The road from Baghdad to Basra is long, bumpy, and boring, but the railway, which remains practically unchanged since it was built by the Germans in the early 20th century to connect the Ottoman Empire with the West, should not be shunned.

The train ride is long, long and then somehow even longer than you imagine and there is much that is unappealing. It will leave late and arrive even later. The boys of every town see the train as target practice for their slingshots. There is little glass in the windows, providing natural air conditioning and a steady flow of stinging dust. You need to bring plenty of water and a wet rag to wipe the layers of mud from your face.

Instead the appeal of the train ride lies in a pace that allows you to sit back and enjoy the stunning scenery and patchwork of characters that have chosen to make the intrepid journey with you.

After nosing its way through the back gardens and streets of Baghdad the train

Baghdad staging-post) will be happy to arrange transport for you. He speaks fluent English, uses regular drivers and will organise shared trips to lower the cost. He can also arrange transport out of Baghdad.

chugs on over five hours of flat desert dotted with Bedouin tents, skinny sheep and dramatically colourful washing lines. The train passes the wet marshes filled with naked boys splashing in the mud pools and fishing for supper on their wobbly rafts. Many Marsh Arabs take advantage of the cheap train ride – a heady 50 cents – to transport their goods to market and if you are lucky they may invite you to lunch. There follows miles of dry marshes, empty mud huts, the occasional black figure in the distance the only sign of life, before you hit Basra.

If someone has not befriended you and insisted you stay at their house for the night by the time you arrive, then head for the Mirbad Hotel – the most secure and expensive place in town. Sadly, it's very hard to find 'luxury' in Basra – and you will be dreaming of it after your 11-hour ordeal of a journey.

According to Ahmed, the train conductor of 27 years, 'the Americans have promised seven more trains'. Where they would fit them on the single track with only the one crossover point he could not answer. Then again, the last time I took the train the second bomb to hit the line that day blew the 'down-train' off the tracks at Babylon, so perhaps some spares are needed.

Prices fluctuate wildly according to the security and petrol situation. Expect to pay around US$200–250 for an entire GMC and US$150 for a car from the al-Saraya in normal circumstances, more from the Hotel Intercontinental.

al-Saraya Hotel Downtown, Amman; tel: +9626 465 6791; fax: +9626 465 6792; email: saraya-hotel@index.com.jo

Hotel Intercontinental Queen Zein St, Jabal Amman; tel: +9626 464 1361

There are cheaper alternatives, for the more intrepid. Orange-and-white Iraqi taxis (both cars and GMCs) now regularly ply the route, many drivers doing the journey every day. Few taxis now wait at the border, preferring to make time by driving through the night. The Jordanian government has a strict vetting process for taxi drivers, but caution should be exercised while the threat of kidnap remains.

A place in a GMC will set you back around US$20–30, but be prepared to haggle. You will also have to sit around until the taxi is full unless you are prepared to pay for the extra seats. Taxis leave Amman from al-Mahtta bus station, in Downtown Amman (if you go to Abdali bus station it will be more expensive). GMC taxis leave Baghdad from the intersection of Rasheed Street and Ahrar Bridge Street in Rusafa. Cars leave Baghdad from the northern bus station (see map, F5), near to the central railway station in the Karkh district. Taxis for Baghdad will normally leave in the early evening, those for Jordan will leave first thing in the morning.

The Jet bus has a daily shuttle from al-Mahtta bus station in Amman to the northern bus station in Baghdad. At around US$8 this is by far the cheapest option and a great introduction to Iraqi bonhomie. Book a day in advance from the bus station; buses go twice-daily.

By air

At present two main airlines fly to Baghdad International Airport from Amman: Royal Jordanian and Air Serv. The flight takes around two hours. Neither company has a fixed schedule and competition for seats is high.

There have been rocket attacks against aircraft and the descent is always a point of comment. On cloudy days the aeroplane uses the cover as a visual shield for as long as possible and the final descent is extremely steep; on clear days the aeroplane rocks from side to side to make targeting less easy.

Royal Jordanian www.rja.com.jo. *Baghdad*: Ground floor, Conference Centre; tel: +9641 816 6077/6088; email: BGWGARJ@rja.com.jo. *Amman*: Hotel Intercontinental, Jabal Amman; tel: +9626 464 4267; email: AMMTJRJ@rja.com.jo. *Fares*: Tier 1 (CPA, Iraqi officials on duty): US$250 (single), US$515 (return). Tier 2 (Contractors, press, businessmen, others): US$550 (single), US$1,115 (return).

Air Serv www.airserv.org; email: jordan@airserv.org. At least one flight goes per day, but you have to be a certified NGO to get on. US$165 (single).

UNHAS email: iraq.unhas@wfp.org. Runs flights a few times a week, primarily for NGOs. Complete Iraq-specific information is available at www.unjlc.org/content/index.phtml/itemId/8513

Alternative routes

Entry through **Kuwait** is a good alternative to the usual Jordanian route. Kuwait City is 554km from Baghdad. Be aware of strict visa entry and exit requirements, for failure to comply can lead to massive delays. Contact your local Kuwaiti embassy. Note that those with Israeli stamps may be refused entry.

Entering or leaving the country from **Syria** can be a bureaucratic nightmare. Ensure that you have a full, valid Syrian visa before attempting to cross the border. The Tal Kochal crossing is believed to be the safest, as further south there is an increased threat from bandits. Al-Tanf/al-Waleed is the normal crossing when travelling from Baghdad.

GMC taxis to Damascus (748km) leave Baghdad from the intersection of Rasheed Street and Ahrar Bridge Street in Rusafa and cost around US$20–35 per place. Cars and buses leave from the northern bus station, near to the central railway station in the Karkh district.

Entry into Iraq is possible from **Turkey** and for those looking to drive from Europe, this is the most practical entrance. The mountain passes are reputedly stunning. To cross at the Habur border requires special permission from the Turkish government and must be arranged a minimum of 10 days in advance through the Ministry of Foreign Affairs – International Political Institutions Headquarters.

It is possible to journey to and from Iraq by **boat**, but this will require some planning. Several passenger ferries now operate between Dubai and Umm Qasr although conditions are reported to be extremely basic. The three-day voyage costs US$170. Romantics can even hire a dhow to journey from Dubai. Once in Basra taxis and buses leave regularly for Baghdad (445km) and arrive and depart from Baghdad's southern bus station in Rusafa, on the intersection of Sheik Omar Street and Thawra Street, near to the expressway.

Access via Saudi Arabia and Iran is not possible.

By train

Baghdad station is worth a visit in itself with a huge marble booking hall. Trains leave for Basra and Mosul at around 8.00am and cost a trifling ID2000 per ticket. The train is exceptionally slow and exceptionally hot. There have also been explosions on the line. From Mosul there are weekly trains to Aleppo in Syria.

HEALTH

Make sure that you have a thorough medical and dental examination before travelling to Baghdad, and that you have an adequate supply of any medication that you take regularly. Although medicine is available in the capital, it is certainly worth bringing a selection of basics including anti-diarrhoea tablets.

Most people who visit Baghdad for the first time will come down with the ubiquitous Baghdad-belly. Often it is simply a reaction to the change in food and water, but be careful to wash and cook food thoroughly before consumption. Make sure that you drink plenty of water and seek medical attention for any prolonged attack. The most common and particularly nasty form lasts approximately 36–48 hours and includes diarrhoea, vomiting, fever and occasionally slight delirium.

While the local population drink the tap water, which was originally fit for human consumption, the damage done to the water system both in the 1991 Gulf War and the recent conflict means that it is no longer advisable, if at all possible. While not something you should make a regular habit, courtesy may force you to drink water that you would otherwise avoid. Most people have found themselves in this predicament and you will be unlucky if you notice any side effects. The mineral content of Baghdad water is particularly high and kidney stones are a common problem in the city, even among the young.

The frenetic post-war looting spree even extended to sewage plants and even the best areas are sometimes bathed in fetid pools of rising sewage. As a result, it is essential that any open cuts on your feet or legs are both regularly sterilised and kept well covered. It is worth having a bottle of iodine solution or similar disinfectant to hand in case you cut yourself. Iraqis are meticulous about the most minor cuts and grazes.

There are several vaccinations or boosters that the British NHS recommends you have before any travel to Iraq

Diphtheria Spread through close respiratory contact.

Hepatitis A A faecal/oral infection spread through contaminated food or water.

Poliomyelitis Spread mainly through faecally contaminated food and water.

Tetanus Contracted through dirty cuts and scratches.

Typhoid A faecal/oral infection spread through contaminated food and water.

For those travelling to Baghdad for longer periods of time, or working in high-risk situations, the following further vaccines are recommended.

Planning

Hepatitis B Spread through blood, blood products and sexual intercourse. The vaccination is a course and so you must contact your doctor at least four weeks in advance if you think you will need the vaccination. Carriage of the virus among the population in Iraq is believed to be medium (2–10%).

Rabies Spread through saliva of infected animals. Recommended for anyone travelling more than 24 hours from a reliable source of vaccine and for those with frequent animal contact. A course of three doses, given over a four-week period, is considered more effective. In the case of a bite, at least one booster should still be sought.

Meningitis Vaccination with a single dose of the tetravalent vaccine meningitis ACWY may be recommended for travellers who will be working in close contact with the local population and are intending to spend a long period of time in Baghdad.

Tuberculosis Spread through close respiratory contact and occasionally through infected milk or milk products. TB is common and BCG is recommended for anyone mixing closely with the local population.

Malaria Those who remain in Baghdad are not considered at risk, although it is certainly worth bringing mosquito repellent as the summer months can be torturous otherwise. The greatest risk is from benign malaria between May and November in the northern regions below 1,500m and in the swamp areas around Basra in the south. Chloroquine is recommended for those visiting risk areas during the transmission season.

Health

Other diseases to be aware of:

Leishmaniasis Spread through the bite of an infected sandfly. It can cause a slow-growing skin lump or ulcer (cutaneous form) and sometimes a life-threatening fever with weight-loss and anaemia (Kala-azar). Infected dogs are carriers. There was a particularly severe outbreak of the latter in April 2003 with UNICEF announcing more than 200 cases. The risk is much higher outside Baghdad.

Schistosomiasis (Bilharzias) Spread through the fresh-water snail. Caused by a fluke, it leads to infection of the bowel and bladder, often accompanied by bleeding. It's contracted through the skin from water contaminated with human urine or faeces. Paddling or swimming in suspect fresh-water lakes or slow-running rivers should be avoided.

It is worth noting that the CPA medical clinic is still offering staff vaccination against both anthrax and smallpox.

Blood

Before the looting left hospitals bare, there was a fully stocked haematology lab and blood was screened before use. This has been destroyed and you should now be extremely sceptical about receiving blood from an unknown source. Although there is a relatively low incidence of the HIV virus in Iraq, all cases were brought to Baghdad and the patients, many of whom remain ignorant about the nature of their disease, have returned to the streets. Vials of contaminated blood were stolen from

Planning

labs after the war and have not been recovered. There is also a risk of Hepatitis B. Iraqis have taken to using their friends and relatives for direct transfusions, a practice worth considering. You should know your blood type before travelling.

Travel clinics and health information

A full list of current travel clinic websites worldwide is available on www.istm.org/. For other journey preparation information, consult www.tripprep.com. Information about various medications may be found on www.emedicine.com/wild/topiclist.htm.

UK

Berkeley Travel Clinic 32 Berkeley St, London W1J 8EL (near Green Park tube station); tel: 020 7629 6233

British Airways Travel Clinic and Immunisation Service There are two BA clinics in London, both on tel: 0845 600 2236; web: www.britishairways.com/travel/HEALTHCLININTRO. Appointments only at 101 Cheapside; or walk-in service Mon–Sat at 213 Piccadilly. Apart from providing inoculations and malaria prevention, they sell a variety of health-related goods.

Cambridge Travel Clinic 48a Mill Rd, Cambridge CB1 2AS; tel: 01223 367362; fax: 01223 368021; email: mkedward@cambridgetravelclinic.co.uk; web: www.cambridgetravelclinic.co.uk. Open 12.00–19.00 Tue–Fri, 10.00–16.00 Sat.

Edinburgh Travel Clinic Regional Infectious Diseases Unit, Ward 41 OPD, Western General Hospital, Crewe Rd South, Edinburgh EH4 2UX; tel: 0131 537 2822. Travel helpline

Health

AIDS

Ask someone on the streets of Baghdad what they think of AIDS in Iraq. Some will be smug, others indignant, but the response will almost always be the same – there is no AIDS in Iraq.

The compulsory AIDS test for all visitors to Iraq added credence to the belief that Iraq remained free from HIV, but in reality the sole value of the test was to bolster such propaganda. Before the war, one journalist said he had been asked to pay US$50 to receive the test or US$100 to avoid it. He paid US$100. Such stories abound, and for those who agreed to the test, the central records proved easy to falsify for the appropriate fee.

The high-security hospital on the outskirts of Baghdad in which HIV+ patients were housed ensured the public ignorance of their existence. Once inside the HIV ward of Ibn Zuhor, the TB hospital, they ceased to exist. Kept under 24-hour guard their presence remained a well-kept secret. Even resident doctors were not cleared to enter the ward. Their only contact with the outside world was specialist doctors and one nurse, who without specific training in handling AIDS patients believed that the HIV virus could be contracted by touch.

open 09.00–12.00 weekdays. Provides inoculations and anti-malarial prophylaxis and advises on travel-related health risks.

In 2002 under international pressure HIV+ patients who were also haemophiliac were released after signing a contract that effectively placed them under house arrest (this included children who wanted to pursue their education).

During the post-war pillaging Ibn Zuhor was torn down by looters. Of the patients who disappeared during the frenzy, all are believed to be sexually active and the majority were prostitutes likely to return to their former trade. Intended to have been incarcerated until their death, they have not received any education about their condition nor how to avoid spreading it further. In a city convinced that AIDS does not exist, their partners will be unlikely to take appropriate precautions or even know what those might be.

Several organisations, including the Red Crescent and the International Medical Corp, are involved in education programmes.

AIDS came to Iraq in 1986 when a group of young haemophiliacs were given tainted blood products. The French company implicated in the scandal was sued for $3million damages, but sanctions forced the case out of court and the compensation claim remains unresolved. Efforts have been renewed since the fall of Saddam to force a settlement.

Fleet Street Travel Clinic 29 Fleet St, London EC4Y 1AA; tel: 020 7353 5678; web: www.fleetstreet.com. Injections, travel products and latest advice.

Health

Hospital for Tropical Diseases Travel Clinic Mortimer Market Centre, 2nd Floor, Capper St (off Tottenham Ct Rd), London WC1E 6AU; tel: 020 7388 9600; web: www.thehtd.org. Offers consultations and advice, and is able to provide all necessary drugs and vaccines for travellers. Runs a healthline (09061 337733) for country-specific information and health hazards. Also stocks nets, water purification equipment and personal protection measures.

MASTA (Medical Advisory Service for Travellers Abroad), at the London School of Hygiene and Tropical Medicine, Keppel St, London WC1 7HT; tel: 09068 224100. This is a premium-line number, charged at 60p per minute. For a fee, they will provide an individually tailored health brief, with up-to-date information on how to stay healthy, inoculations and what to bring.

MASTA pre-travel clinics Tel: 01276 685040. Call for the nearest; there are currently 30 in Britain. Also sell malaria prophylaxis memory cards, treatment kits, bednets, net treatment kits.

NHS travel website www.fitfortravel.scot.nhs.uk, provides country-by-country advice on immunisation and malaria, plus details of recent developments, and a list of relevant health organisations.

Nomad Travel Store 3–4 Wellington Terrace, Turnpike Lane, London N8 0PX; tel: 020 8889 7014; fax: 020 8889 9528; email: sales@nomadtravel.co.uk; web: www.nomadtravel.co.uk. Also at 40 Bernard St, London WC1N 1LJ; tel: 020 7833 4114; fax: 020 7833 4470 and 43 Queens Rd, Bristol BS8 1QH; tel: 0117 922 6567; fax: 0117 922 7789. As well as dispensing health advice, Nomad stocks mosquito nets and other anti-bug devices, and an excellent range of adventure travel gear.

Thames Medical 157 Waterloo Rd, London SE1 8US; tel: 020 7902 9000. Competitively priced, one-stop travel health service. All profits go to their affiliated company, InterHealth, which provides health care for overseas workers on Christian projects.

Trailfinders Immunisation Centre 194 Kensington High St, London W8 7RG; tel: 020 7938 3999.

Travelpharm www.travelpharm.com offers up-to-date guidance on travel-related health and has a range of medications available through their online mini-pharmacy.

Irish Republic

Tropical Medical Bureau Grafton Street Medical Centre, Grafton Buildings, 34 Grafton St, Dublin 2; tel: 1 671 9200. Has a useful website specific to tropical destinations: www.tmb.ie.

USA

Centers for Disease Control 1600 Clifton Rd, Atlanta, GA 30333; tel: 888 232 3228 (toll free and available 24 hours) or 800 311 3435; fax: 877 FYI TRIP; web: www.cdc.gov/travel. The central source of travel information in the USA. Each summer they publish the invaluable Health Information for International Travel, available from the Division of Quarantine at the above address.

Connaught Laboratories PO Box 187, Swiftwater, PA 18370; tel: 800 822 2463. They will send a free list of specialist tropical-medicine physicians in your state.

IAMAT (International Association for Medical Assistance to Travelers) 417 Center St, Lewiston, NY 14092; tel: 716 754 4883; email: info@iamat.org; web: www.iamat.org. A non-profit organisation that provides lists of English-speaking doctors abroad.

Health

Canada

IAMAT (International Association for Medical Assistance to Travellers) Suite 1, 1287 St Clair Av W, Toronto, Ontario M6E 1B8; tel: 416 652 0137; web: www.iamat.org
TMVC (Travel Doctors Group) Sulphur Springs Rd, Ancaster, Ontario; tel: 905 648 1112; web: www.tmvc.com.au

Australia, New Zealand, Thailand

TMVC Tel: 1300 65 88 44; web: www.tmvc.com.au. Twenty-two clinics in Australia, New Zealand and Thailand, including:
Auckland Canterbury Arcade, 170 Queen St, Auckland; tel: 9 373 3531
Brisbane Dr Deborah Mills, Qantas Domestic Building, 6th floor, 247 Adelaide St, Brisbane, QLD 4000; tel: 7 3221 9066; fax: 7 3321 7076
Melbourne Dr Sonny Lau, 393 Little Bourke St, 2nd floor, Melbourne, VIC 3000; tel: 3 9602 5788; fax: 3 9670 8394
Sydney Dr Mandy Hu, Dymocks Building, 7th Floor, 428 George St, Sydney, NSW 2000; tel: 2 221 7133; fax: 2 221 8401
IAMAT PO Box 5049, Christchurch 5, New Zealand; web: www.iamat.org

South Africa

SAA-Netcare Travel Clinics PO Box 786692, Sandton 2146; fax: 011 883 6152; web: www.travelclinic.co.za or www.malaria.co.za. Clinics throughout South Africa.
TMVC 113 DF Malan Drive, Roosevelt Park, Johannesburg; tel: 011 888 7488; web: www.tmvc.com.au. Consult the website for details of clinics in South Africa.

Planning

SAFETY

Until the security situation is fully under control, personal safety will remain the gravest concern for anyone visiting Baghdad and should be taken exceptionally seriously. Adequate planning is essential and any visitor should ensure that they are well appraised of the current security situation prior to arrival. Consider taking a security course before departing.

All foreign nationals should register with their diplomatic mission on arrival (see *Chapter 14*, and page 178). Up-to-date travel advice is available on the UK FCO website (www.fco.gov.uk); for the time being the FCO is expected to continue advising against all non-essential travel to Iraq. The latest US advice is available on www.travel.state.gov and detailed security information is available at http://www.centcom.mil and security.advisor@us.army.mil

The specific security situation changes on a daily basis. For NGO workers, a daily spot report is available from NCCI, www.ncciraq.org (see page 187).

More generally, there are trends in the primary threat to foreign nationals in Iraq. In summer 2003 the greatest concern centred around random shootings. Subsequently, attacks against foreign targets have become more sophisticated and include car bombs, mortars, rockets, rocket-propelled grenades (RPGs) and walking suicide bombers in addition to the perennial threat from small-arms fire. The perpetrators are inventive; rocket attacks have been launched from donkey carts and improvised explosive devices (IEDs) are often placed in dead animals, pot holes or rubbish. From early 2004 the kidnap, and in some cases subsequent

IMPORTANT NOTE

The safety section in this guide in no way attempts to provide a substitute for professional, and up-to-the-minute security advice. Anyone visiting Iraq while the security situation remains highly volatile is advised to seek current, professional advice prior to, and throughout, their stay.

While ever kidnap remains a primary tactic of the insurgent movement, exposure should be kept to an *absolute minimum*. Accommodation must be adequately guarded and only limited, essential journeys made outside. When these are unavoidable, the route should be planned before leaving your accommodation, taking into consideration known traffic delays and avoiding volatile areas of town. Some have taken to sitting in the back seat, obscured by drawn curtains. Remain as secretive as possible about any trip prior to its

beheading, of foreigners became the latest gruesome twist in the security nightmare faced by anyone visiting Baghdad.

When, and only when, the general security situation allows for travel around the city, the simplest advice is to blend in as much as possible. For women this may mean adopting local dress. Men who intend to walk the streets unprotected should aim to look as un-military as possible. Consider growing facial hair and avoid close, military-style haircuts, although excessively long hair will attract unwanted attention.

Planning

event. On departure, inform someone you trust of your intended whereabouts and the approximate duration of the excursion. Do not walk around in public areas. Eat in your place of residence. This applies to *all* foreign nationals, including those previously considered at lower risk from other forms of opportunistic attack. The sudden change in tactics in early 2004, and its spread, serves to highlight the importance of up-to-date security information.

All visitors to Baghdad should keep a supply of hard currency sufficient to get them out of the country in an emergency. Plan in advance what measure you intend to take should evacuation prove necessary. It is advisable to negotiate a 'safe-house' in case the situation deteriorates rapidly and safe removal from the city prove impossible.

Many of the larger organisations have rigid rules determining the type of vehicle that staff must use, but the same rule of understatement applies. If you have the choice, aim to travel around the city in a nondescript car. While it is important that the engine be in good condition and that it will not breakdown, a few scratches and some (even severe) cosmetic damage will help you to blend in more completely. This is particularly important if you are obliged to visit the less-salubrious quarters of Baghdad.

Safety

Places where Westerners are known to congregate such as restaurants and hotels are at increased risk of attack, as are official buildings, police stations, military installations and CPA-administered sites. The entrances to the Green Zone have been attacked on a number of occasions.

In addition to maintaining a low profile, a few other security points should be followed. These are not intended to be complete; they are no more than guidelines to appropriate behaviour.

- Always obey those designated to safeguard your security; do not think that you know better, no matter how infuriating the proscriptions may be. If you do not have professional security personnel and are unsure about an area of Baghdad or a trip you intend to make, then ask around (hotel receptions, translators and fellow foreigners). Remember that the answer to 'How safe will I be?' is a matter of opinion, so make sure you ask people you trust or whose views on acceptable risk most closely match your own. A spectrum of justified opinion can help.
- Be accompanied at all times by someone who speaks Arabic fluently and who knows the city well. They will be able to read the mood of situations and know which areas to avoid. Always listen to them, even if their reticence or demands (additional clothing, for example) seem unreasonable. They may be the only person between you and a potential attacker and they are less likely to assist if difficulties arise after you have defied their better judgement.

Planning

- Always inform someone of your movements and what time you expect to return. This is especially important if you make frequent trips out of Baghdad.
- Keep a functioning telephone with you at all times.
- Do not go out with large quantities of money. The money you do carry should be kept in a bum-bag under clothing or in a zipped handbag. Leave expensive accessories in your room or in a safe; those you have to carry (cameras, satellite phones etc) should be kept out of sight.
- Keep away from crowds, especially avoiding demonstrations. Keep visits to public buildings and police stations to a minimum. Do not loiter around checkpoints and always allow military convoys to overtake. Avoid driving abreast official vehicles.
- The 23.00 curfew was lifted in October 2003, but you should still be exceptionally careful when driving at night and keep a close lookout for checkpoints, which sometimes seem to appear out of nowhere. On the approach to a checkpoint slow down to a walking pace, dim headlights and turn on any internal lights. Avoid making any fast or unnecessary hand movements – if possible, keep your hands visible at all times. Obey any instructions given immediately.
- If you are obliged to visit dangerous sectors of the city, avoid eye contact, walk purposefully and walk slightly in front of your guide. You are the conspicuous target and most foreigners have been shot from behind. Keep photography to an absolute minimum unless you are a clearly marked press photographer.

- Do not linger in the street; if you have to, wait in front of a wall or a tree with your back to it.
- Never walk around after dark. It is inadvisable to walk in Betaween, Shorjah and Sadr City (although you should check the local situations on your arrival and the caution is by no means limited to these), and you should never be in such areas out of broad daylight.
- Don't take taxis on your own, certainly not if you are a woman. If stuck, choose a taxi driven by an old man.
- When relaxing indoors, keep as far away from the road, the entrance and glass windows as possible.

At the moment there are no designated emergency numbers, although civil defence hotline 115 should soon become operative. You should go to the press desk and the Iraqi Assistance Centre, in the Conference Centre, for updated military/security numbers as soon as you arrive.

Women

If you are a foreign woman coming to Baghdad then you'll be joining a distinct minority. Quite how few women come to Baghdad was highlighted before a press conference given by Donald Rumsfeld. The press hall was bursting with the world's media and as an additional security measure men and women were asked to line up in two queues to be searched, while sniffer-dogs scoured the hall. The 15 or so women smugly and swiftly got back to their seats while the men's queue snaked away to the end the long corridor. One veteran, bound for the back of the queue, was clearly heard to mutter, 'Who on earth said there was a feminisation of the media!'

Western women, especially those with light hair, elicit a fair amount of attention. That said, most of it is harmless. Wolf-whistling, groping and all the other common unpleasantries of being a woman abroad are not usually a problem in Baghdad and as long as you don't speak Arabic you won't know what's being said about you.

Unfortunately, single women are often viewed as prostitutes and if you go out for a meal with a man, especially a local man, expect to be stared at. Among the myriad newspapers to spring up are a number of gutter publications that are not beyond writing hate articles about 'Western whorehouses', happily including directions, which will inevitably lead to the office of a Western NGO or business employing female workers.

While these are the obvious downsides to being a woman in Baghdad, there are clear advantages too. The greatest is the ability to 'disappear' by donning local dress; all but the most fair will fit into the range of complexion found in Iraq. If you are prepared to do so, you may feel able to visit areas that are otherwise off limits.

There are three types of local dress: Western clothing (usually synthetic, highly patterned and in dark colours) with a scarf, the *hijab* and the bat-like *abaya*. Almost no one walks around with her face completely covered. You must wear a headscarf that fully covers your hair when visiting a mosque and an *abaya* to visit a Shia shrine.

The issue of the headscarf is a sensitive one. The majority of Western women in Baghdad choose not to wear one but if you do, you may find yourself treated with markedly more respect.

The flipside is that the Christian community and some liberal Muslims will strongly object, a few even refusing to speak to you until you remove the veil once they know you are not Muslim. There are many Westernised women in the city who now feel obliged to wear the veil for security reasons, and many who still refuse to, but feel under increasing pressure. These groups and the men who agree with them feel strongly that Western women should support the right of women to walk the street bareheaded.

Women should fully cover the torso and limbs when in public and avoid wearing tight clothing. Ask your translator if he finds your attire appropriate; if not, listen to him. There have been unfortunate reports of translators refusing to intervene in unpleasant situations because they felt the woman had 'brought it on herself'. In one case the victim was wearing loose jeans, so do not assume that your idea of demure is sufficient.

Women should never walk in public areas on their own and should preferably always be accompanied by a man. Do not take taxis alone. In the current security state, when Iraqi women are behind the wheel they will almost always be accompanied and they do not drive after dark without a male chaperone.

Mine awareness

Provided by the National Mine Action Authority (Iraq)

As a result of 20 years of wars and bombing campaigns and little in the way of clean-up operations, Iraq is very heavily contaminated with landmines, unexploded ordinance (UXO) and abandoned munitions. Many of these are hidden or, in the case of the large and highly volatile missiles that litter the roadsides on the way out of Baghdad, may present the illusion of being harmless. All pose an extreme threat to the public and certain basic precautions should be taken by anyone visiting Baghdad or Iraq.

- Keep to known, safe paths and if possible to tarmac roads. Don't park off the sides of roads.
- Clues about the presence of mines include: dead animals, craters, packing cases, spools of wire, visible mines, military positions, abandoned vehicles with tracks/wheels blown off, remnants of wire fences, official marking signs (red triangle), local or other marking systems, unused agricultural land.
- Do not enter abandoned buildings, abandoned military vehicles (such as tanks), military sites or known battle areas.

Safety

LANDMINES AND UNEXPLODED ORDNANCE (UXO)

Decades of intermittent external and internal conflict and a long, cross-border territorial war with Iran has left Iraq ranked among some of the most landmine and unexploded ordnance contaminated countries in the world, alongside other conflict-affected nations as Afghanistan and Angola.

In addition, minefields lying along the 'green line', which separates central Iraq from the three northern, Kurdish-controlled Governorates, constitute a physical barrier between two factions within a new Iraq.

During the recent conflict, the former regime left caches of arms and munitions stockpiled throughout the country creating a real and constant danger to the civilian community. Bombs with sub-munitions (containing hundreds of smaller bomblets) were dropped on Iraq by Coalition aircraft during the last invasion and around 15% of the small bomblets failed to detonate, adding to the contamination.

These small bombs remain where they fell, detonating at the slightest disturbance – often with fatal consequences. Cleaning up explosive remnants of war is both a dangerous and costly business. Most munitions are buried below the ground's surface and are difficult to locate, lying in wait for unsuspecting victims.

These explosive remnants of war not only affect individuals' general health, but there are social, environmental and economic impacts too. The net result is a serious stumbling block to national reconstruction and development.

Landmines and unexploded bombs in rural areas reduce potential farming regions, while unexploded ordnance fallen on oil fields and industrial areas, requires removal before work can safely begin again.

In 2003, Iraq took the positive step of setting up the National Mine Action Authority within the Ministry of Planning to co-ordinate all mine and UXO clearance operations. Both the Iraqi government and the international donor community have taken this task seriously, providing millions of dollars in funding to develop mine action infrastructure to deal with the monumental problem.

In conjunction with the civil defence and international de-mining organisations, the NMAA set up mine and UXO Clearance Teams complete with mechanical clearance devices, explosives sniffer-dogs and de-mining specialists, to remove explosive remnants of war, make safe dangerous areas, carry out surveys and assessments, and provide Mine Risk Education to those at risk.

However, many of the maps detailing the mined areas are lost or destroyed, making the cleanup process difficult and the task will take decades to complete.

continued overleaf

Safety

LANDMINES ...   *continued from overleaf*

Organizations, companies, investors or visitors should be mindful that these hazards exist and be mine-UXO aware while travelling and working in Iraq.

Individuals or organizations wishing to contribute to this humanitarian effort should co-ordinate their efforts through the National Mine Action Authority.

For more information, the NMAA can be contacted through their website, www.iraqmineaction.org. For emergency response, please call the Iraqi Civil Defence emergency number on 115.

- Do not touch, kick, burn or tamper with any munitions. And don't take them home as souvenirs (a Japanese journalist did just that and ended up killing a customs officer at Amman Airport).
- Gather as much information as you can before you make your trip. However, just because a local resident says an area is safe, don't assume it is. It is possible that they do not know themselves, or that they are prepared to take unacceptable risks.
- Avoid rubbish and dead animals in the road as they may be concealing improvised explosive devices intended to target the Coalition forces or their allies.
- If you find a strange object, leave it alone – it could be a booby trap.

- If you get stuck in a minefield, don't move. Shout for help but tell others to stay away. Ask someone to contact the Civil Defence, police or military. Do not try to enter a minefield to rescue someone, even if they are injured. The rescue team will have to de-mine a safe path.

Weapons

Weapons' authorisation is available from the Ministry of the Interior. For weapons' legislation, at the time of writing, see CPA Order 3 and Memorandum 100 (http://www.iraqcoalition.org/regulations/index.html).

If you are thinking of living in private accommodation, you should certainly hire a guard, particularly at night. In reality few Westerners, other than security personnel and some contractors, carry weapons.

When considering whether or not to arm it is particularly important to note that a weapon is not of itself a deterrent in Baghdad. This is not Europe, where showing a gun may cause an opportunistic criminal to turn tail: anyone threatening you will almost certainly be armed and the sight of a weapon may prompt them to use their own. If you carry a gun you must be prepared to use it. If you are prepared to, then a further word of warning: Iraq is still a tribal society where reprisal is a point of honour and as a foreigner you have no tribe to protect you from, or to negotiate, the consequences. Note that it is illegal to shoot anyone not physically on your property; only a warning shot may be fired. You should receive appropriate training before buying a weapon.

WHAT TO BRING

What you bring will very much depend on the length of your stay. Certainly it is worth bringing a radio, torch, good (but not flashy) watch, alarm clock, some hard-wearing shoes, a bum-bag and an everyday bag that both closes properly and is large enough to hold a satellite phone.

Surprisingly, most things are available in Baghdad. The borders were leaky under sanctions and imports have been flooding the market since they were lifted. Endless lines of lorries transporting cars and electrical goods clog the Jordanian border-crossing each morning, and the selection of electronic items is excellent as a result.

Toiletries are also readily available, but a supply of shampoo and conditioner is useful as the local formulas are not always suitable for Western hair. Sun cream is a good idea in the summer, particularly for fairer skins, and is not widely sold in Baghdad. Women should remember to bring sanitary products as only basics are available.

In the summer mosquitoes come forth in their thousands. While those found in Baghdad do not carry malaria (unlike the mosquitoes of the southern marshes around Basra) they are fully capable of making your life miserable. Bring an adequate supply of insect-repellent and soothing antihistamine creams. Unless you know you will be sleeping in a fully air-conditioned bedroom do not bother with a mosquito net – you'll need every breath of air to get to sleep.

You should bring sufficient cool, cotton clothing and underwear to see you through the summer months. Clothes made with natural fibres are expensive and relatively hard to find, although some hotel shops sell a small selection of trousers and shirts.

While sunglasses are available, you should bring a good pair with high UV protection. Don't forget your bathing costume, for a dip in a hotel pool is one of the nicest ways to cool down. Bikinis are acceptable in some hotels but bring an alternative.

If you are to stay in Baghdad for any length of time a good supply of books, DVDs and CDs are essential as the local selection is poor to non-existent (pirated copies, although freely available, are usually of terrible quality). Try to bring books that you are happy to leave behind: Iraqis have been starved of Western literature for over a decade and are exceptionally grateful for anything to read.

MONEY

On October 15 2003, the new Iraqi dinar came in to circulation, replacing the 'Swiss' dinar in Kurdistan and the 'print' or 'Saddam' dinar in the rest of Iraq. After a changeover period, the new dinar became the only legal currency on January 15 2004. The new dinar comes in six denominations from ID50 to ID25,000 and is of a completely new design – gone is Saddam's beaming face.

While many in Kurdistan were sad to say goodbye to the 'Swiss' dinar (originally circulated throughout Iraq, but kept on in the north after 1991), the rest of Iraq breathed a sigh of relief. The Iraqi dinar had seen astonishing inflation over the last twenty years. In 1982 the then value of the Iraqi dinar, US$1 = ID0.31, became the unflinching official exchange rate, unchanged until the fall of Baghdad in April 2003. In reality the real value of the dinar shortly before the war had plummeted to around US$1 = ID4,000.

Money

To make matters worse, rumour spread that printing presses had been looted in the aftermath of the conflict and the ID10,000 note fell to 70–80% of its face value, leaving many Iraqis with a severe cash shortage. One of the few places where ID10,000 were in regular use was Baghdad racetrack, where rich punters could be seen blowing stacks of the unwanted notes. Government employees, insisting that they be paid in ID250 notes, left with sacks full of money, and shopping trips would end with the lengthy counting and recounting of wads of notes.

This sudden demand for ID250 notes lead to a nationwide shortage and Coalition Provisional Authority head, Paul Bremer, was forced to make the embarrassing decision to print a new run – complete with Saddam's head – in direct contravention of his own rule prohibiting the public reproduction of the former dictator's likeness.

For larger items, hotels and salaries the US dollar is still the accepted form of payment, so it is worth bringing in a supply.

Cash is the only form of payment accepted in Iraq at the moment. Most Iraqis have never even seen a credit or debit card before and producing one can create something of a stir as it gets handed round for inspection before being returned, often with a profound air of disbelief.

There are at present no restrictions on bringing money into Iraq.

Budgeting

Few people can get round the city without hiring a translator-driver and if you look foreign and speak no Arabic it would also be highly inadvisable to try to do so. Although government employees earn under US$100 per month the ceiling was blown off the translator market by the sudden influx of rich news organisations willing to pay anything for good translators. The result means that many ministries and local organisations have found it impossible to employ the English-speaking staff they need. Although prices have begun to settle it is still hard to find a translator-driver for under US$100 per week. For high-quality translation expect to pay around US$20–30 per day.

Excluding transport, it is possible to scrape by in Baghdad on a little over US$10 per day. A budget hotel will set you back around US$15 for a double and street food costs virtually nothing. Drinks cost around ID500 for a can and a large bottle of water about the same. For those not on a shoestring, hotels cost US$25–150 per night, depending on what you require and where you want to be. Price is not always an indication of comfort and some of the cheaper hotels provide better rooms than their more expensive, but established, rivals. To eat out in a Western-style restaurant with wine expect to pay around US$10–20 per head; beer costs around US$2 per can in a hotel.

As there is little else to spend your money on in Baghdad, the amount you need above and beyond transport, accommodation and food is almost directly related to the amount of alcohol you wish to drink and what souvenirs you want to buy.

ELECTRICITY

220 volts; AC 50Hz. There is still a national shortage of power, variously blamed on damage inflicted by the post-war looting, an antiquated and crumbling

infrastructure, saboteurs, decentralisation of the supply (Baghdad used to get additional power to the detriment of the provinces) and the increase in demand. Some improvement has been made, but you will still need access to a reliable generator. Fluctuations in power can have a deleterious effect on computers and other electronic goods and batteries never fully recharge. Two-pin continental-style plugs are more common than three-pin UK plugs, although both are found. Adapters and extension cables are easily available.

Uninterrupted power supplies (UPSs) are widely available. Usually connected to computers, they provide a smooth segue from mains power to generator, or vice versa, thereby lowering the risk of data loss when the power goes out. Nonetheless, save frequently and write long emails in Word.

CULTURAL DOS AND DON'TS

If a fee has been negotiated then a tip is not required unless the service has been exemplary; similarly taxi fares do not have to be raised unless you have been severely caught in traffic when a little extra will be greatly appreciated (and often demanded). You should consider tipping anyone who goes out of their way to assist you, by carrying your bags, for example, or showing you around. If you do not require these services then make that very clear from the start.

Despite the obvious want of many citizens, Iraqis can be the most unbelievably coy people. Be very aware of this, especially if you come from a country with a tradition of being straightforward. When making any offers to people, whether it be a tip for having shown you around a palace, a cup of coffee or even sometimes their hard-earned salary, they may refuse it, sometimes three or more times, before very gladly accepting. Do not take these refusals at face value, nor deal with them brashly; it's a game of politeness and to play it out makes people feel more comfortable. Similarly, many feel exceptionally embarrassed about complaining or asking for anything, particularly if you have built up a friendship. Be on the look out for hints.

Of course the above is not universally true. Baghdad is a city on which several thousand 'rich' Westerners have descended and there are those out to make the most they can from it. You will frequently be pestered by beggars, particularly children (which can be distressing), and taxis are notorious for overcharging in the first place and then demanding more. More difficult to deal with are the endless requests for visas, often from close friends who really think you have some power over the process.

Hospitality is a very important part of Middle Eastern culture and to refuse something can be deeply insulting. Unless you can think of an extremely tactful excuse at least try any food and drink offered, even if you are worried about its provenance. Use your judgement though; if, for example, your host offers to open the bottle of wine that has clearly been treasured for years, politely refuse. Take sweets (if Christians perhaps a bottle of wine) for the family if you are invited round for a special meal.

The concept of time in Iraq (as in much of the Middle East) can be infuriating to foreigners with a job to do. Make clear from the start what hours are expected. In a city often brought to a standstill by traffic, meetings rarely start on time and a half-hour leeway is quite normal.

Business is done over endless cups of sugary tea and the peremptory Western manner can easily offend. As a result, setting yourself up in Baghdad can be a lengthy process. A brusque approach will get the job done but win you few friends and in a society where everything is about who knows whom this can be a disadvantage, unless you have sufficient funds not to care. Age brings status, so if you are conspicuously younger make an especial effort to be polite.

Both men and women should dress conservatively and legs and shoulders of either sex should be covered in public.

Don't try to shake hands with a woman wearing a headscarf and if your offer of a handshake to a woman is rejected, don't take offence. Equally, if *you* are wearing a headscarf don't expect men to shake your hand; the appropriate greeting is to place the right hand on the heart.

It is extremely rude to point the soles of your feet at anyone. If you put your feet up or cross your legs so that the ankle is near the knee, make sure that the sole is not pointing at anyone.

GIVING SOMETHING BACK

There is a glut of new Iraqi charities opening up around Baghdad as well as many international organisations. If you want to donate you will have no shortage of causes. But there are simple things that you can do to give something back.

Bring in books that you are happy to leave behind: foreign reading material has always been expensive, in short supply and educated Iraqis are eager to read almost anything.

Iraqis are desperate to learn English too. Spend time talking to guards and hotel staff. Most will have vocabulary lists that they are trying to absorb: just a few moments' help with pronunciation will usually generate an embarrassing profusion of gratitude.

Offer to buy lunch when you eat out: drivers and translators will often feign a lack of hunger because a restaurant is too expensive for them (they will not presume you are paying). They will almost certainly resist but a little *gentle* persuasion will find out whether they were really hungry or not.

If you need to buy household fabrics (curtains, cushions, tablecloths etc) then consider buying them from the Deaf and Dumb Sewing Institute in Masbah (first turning on the left after the German Embassy). They have a retail outlet and will make to measure.

Buy newspapers from the young paperboys weaving in and out of the traffic. They are often providing vital income for their families, as are the little shoeshine boys that cluster round hotel entrances.

The plight of the street children, particularly those who live round the entrance to the Palestine and Sheraton, moves many who see them. Try to resist giving them money as some of them are fighting a drug problem. If you want to help then buy them food, or as one Russian businessman did, leave some money with a local restaurant to feed one or two of them a day for a few weeks.

Giving something back

Local Transport

With few high rises, Baghdad sprawls along both sides of the river with no real nucleus. The hub of modern commerce is nowhere near the Central Bank and the traditional markets, neither is it near the Coalition Provisional Authority's administrative complex. Furthermore, ministries and embassies are dotted all over the place. It is not unusual to spend a day darting backward and forward between suburbs miles and a river apart. A reliable form of transport is therefore essential.

PRIVATE CAR

The safest way to get around Baghdad is to hire a private car. Drivers cluster around the foyers and entrances to all of the major hotels, in particular on Saadoun Street, by the entrance to the Palestine/Sheraton Complex and around the Hamra Hotel.

A personal recommendation is the safest way to hire a driver; ask some of the people staying in your hotel if they know of anyone suitable. If this is unsuccessful, many drivers will have written recommendations on them. The biggest problem is often the safety of their driving skills more than anything else; never hesitate to ask a driver to slow down. Don't be too put off by the state of the car: Iraqi mechanics are also magicians and cars rarely breakdown despite their often lamentable condition.

At current rates you should expect to pay between US$15 and US$40 per day depending on the car's condition and size, the length of employment and whether the driver is also expected to be a translator.

You will need to pay extra for journeys out of Baghdad. How much will be affected by the current price of petrol. Petrol is normally very cheap (by Western standards) but during shortages can increase thirty-fold.

A few foreigners have begun to buy their own cars. While significantly cheaper in the long run, this is only for the brave or the reckless in the current driving conditions. Be aware when buying a car that blackened-in windows are now illegal.

The increase in car ownership and the almost total meltdown of traffic controls mean that driving in Baghdad can be an infuriating experience. Before the war Baghdad had a Westernised traffic system that was rigorously followed. Now cars can be seen blithely driving the wrong way up motorway slip-roads, ploughing over central reservations and reversing down major roads. It is difficult to decide what is most amazing: that anarchy spreads so quickly or that somehow it all seems to work, just about.

Just after the war drivers paid little or no heed to anyone trying to direct traffic, volunteer traffic 'police' were ignored and nearly run-over and the official police fared little better. After a summer of mayhem, Baghdad's drivers began to realise that a little co-operation might actually mean that everyone got where they were going faster. The volunteers became heroes and solipsistic drivers are now more likely to be greeted with anger.

Nevertheless, it is worth timing non-essential journeys according to the traffic. Thursday afternoon and Friday are the best times to travel. Saturday is the worst day to move around the city as congestion reigns throughout the day.

Private car

During the rest of the week traffic is at its heaviest between 08.00–09.00 and 13.30–15.00.

TAXIS

There are three types of official taxi.

Service (shared) taxis, which are white, travel on pre-assigned routes, the sign on the roof indicating their final destination. Unless you speak and read Arabic it is difficult to ascertain where they are going and the lack of flexibility will probably mean you never use them.

Normal taxis are either orange and white or yellow. Orange-and-white taxis are usually older, some of them being quite astonishingly decrepit, chugging around town at a horse's trot. This will seldom matter, though, as long as traffic jams abound.

Yellow taxis are new and therefore much more comfortable, often complete with air conditioning (it's worth noting that radiators, even in brand new cars, cannot cope with the additional heat of air conditioning in summer traffic jams – exactly when most needed) but are more expensive.

If you are travelling in a group of two or more (an essential security precaution), it is worth hailing every car that passes without passengers. With the massive increase in unemployment since the war, many people will happily turn themselves into impromptu taxi drivers and ferry you around for the normal fee.

As a result taxis are prolific during the day, but the numbers fall off sharply with

Local transport

nightfall. After 22.00 you may encounter serious difficulty finding anyone to take you any appreciable distance and will end up paying three or four times the normal fare even if you do.

There is no meter system in Baghdad, so it is important to ascertain the price of your journey before getting in. You should not expect to pay more than ID2,000 within central Baghdad and about ID4,000 to go to the outskirts, although you will invariably be asked for much more. Prices go up slightly after dark and increase the later it gets. Taxi drivers are notorious for demanding more than the negotiated fare, usually for a trumped-up excuse. If you have made the driver wait for you or the traffic has been particularly heavy (and the journey therefore longer) do give a little more than agreed.

BUSES

There is an operational bus system in central Baghdad with red double-deckers, a gift from the Chinese, plying the routes. Buses are neither frequent nor can they run to a reliable schedule in the current traffic situation. Given the resulting waiting time at roadside bus stops, this is not a recommended form of transport.

4 Accommodation

HOTELS

Hotels are mushrooming in Baghdad and as the crisis pushes up room prices, hoteliers are some of the few people making money. As a result, Baghdad is not a cheap place to stay at the moment, even though the most expensive rooms are basic in comparison to their Western equivalents. Cheaper hotels usually cater for Iranian pilgrims, and though some are happy to accommodate Westerners on the rare occasions they have space, others are actively hostile.

In response to both security concerns and price, organisations and individuals are beginning to move out into apartments and houses, where rents have similarly sky-rocketed. You can easily find yourself paying US$1,000 per month for a single-bedroom flat. It is debatable whether private houses or hotel rooms are safer. Concentrations of people can both provide security (against single assassins/armed looters/kidnappers) and increase the likelihood of attack (from organised bombings/RPG attacks).

Unless your organisation has a secure base in the city you should certainly stay at a hotel for the first few days. Even if you move out, you'll probably find much of your time is spent drinking coffee in hotels, simply in order to meet people. The fascinating company available means that you may choose never to leave. If you've no prior plans then head to the al-Finar; it's central, friendly, clean and a meeting place for an eclectic mix of people including journalists, contractors and activists.

Even at the largest hotels prices are not fixed, but vary according to the security situation and the duration of your stay. Don't be scared to discuss the price with the manager or to scout around; if you are staying for several months, prices can often be dramatically reduced.

Make sure you see a room before taking it: room quality can vary enormously and it's easier to complain at the beginning. If you are easily disturbed, don't forget to find out where the generator is.

Remember that price is usually indicative both of the quality of the room and the security offered, so certainly bear the latter in mind before going for the cheapest option. Find out what security measures are in place and also who is staying there. While you should not stay somewhere without other foreign guests, a popular hotel may be at increased risk. Several hotels have been the target of attacks employing both car bombs and rocket-propelled grenades. Remember to draw your curtains at night as they can help shield flying glass.

Don't become paranoid, but even choosing a room involves security considerations:

- Where are the escape routes? An alternative to the stairs could prove useful.
- Is your room near a road? If there is a car bomb, the further away the better.
- What does your room overlook? RPGs have been used against hotels.
- How high is your room? Again this is important in the event of an RPG attack.

Which consideration is the most important will depend on the location, clientele and the security measures in place.

Hotels

A	Top-price, large hotels
B	Top-price, medium/small hotels
C	Mid-price
D	Budget or few Westerners

Saadoun area

This area is perfectly situated for easy access to the CPA complex (on the other side of the river), the Old City and the new commercial centre. The streets are noisy and bustling but increasingly dangerous (at the time of writing) as you move toward Tahrir Square, beyond the Palestine Hotel.

A Hotel Ishtar Sheraton (310 rooms) Firdos Square; tel: 816 00 39/93; fax: 886 3300; email: ishtar@burntmail.com [4 H5]. Founded in 1982 the large number of US companies based in the hotel makes it the busiest in town: occupancy rates are now over 90%. The rooms are clean and spacious, most with good views over the city. The view from the roof is breathtaking, especially at sunset, but permission is required. Facilities include a small swimming pool (free for guests, approximately ID2,000 for non-residents), health club (sauna, steam-room, basic gym and massage – entry US$5 for residents and non-residents), shops selling essentials and souvenirs, a barbers and 24hr internet access. There are two basic cafés and a buffet restaurant (US$10 per meal). The Sheraton (so called by everyone, but no longer part of the chain) has been the target of RPG attacks.
Security: High
Rates: US$100–300 (suite), US$70–80 (normal), including breakfast.

Accommodation

A Hotel Palestine (408 rooms) Firdos Square; tel: 747 0874/5678 [4 H5]. Founded in 1982, the Palestine is famous for housing journalists during the last conflict and many news corporations are still based here. With a cosier feel than the echoing Sheraton, the Palestine rooms are spacious if a little drab. Facilities include a pool complex, a health club (ID2,000–3,000 per day or annual membership for ID80,000–100,000), shops selling essentials and souvenirs and internet access. Tennis courts and a bowling alley are under renovation. There are two cafés and two restaurants, the outdoor barbeque is a great place to dine, particularly in the summer, when they serve fish so fresh that they are swimming in the garden's fountain moments before you eat them. Like the Sheraton, the Palestine has been subject to RPG attack.

Security: High

Rates: US$110–160 (suite), US$70–90 (normal), including breakfast

A al-Sadeer Hotel (278 rooms) Andalus Square, next to Ministry of Agriculture [4 H5]. In the process of being refurbished, the al-Sadeer will aim to rival the nearby Sheraton and Palestine hotels, sporting a swimming pool, gym, restaurant, bar and business centre. At the moment no further details are available.

B Hotel al-Finar (40 rooms) Abu Newas, by the entrance to the Sheraton [CC]. The al-Finar is almost certainly the best value for money in Baghdad. The staff are friendly and the British-Iraqi owner knows what Western visitors want. The first-floor restaurant and ground-floor coffee shop have been refurbished in the traditional style with bright woollen rugs, wooden benches with large cushions and pillars rescued from old Baghdadi houses. The rooms are relatively large, with a balcony, but each one is differently furnished and

Hotels

draped, so if you don't like the one you're shown look at some others. The charmingly eccentric atmosphere is completed by a parrot, Coco, who happily chatters away to guests in the reception (and could apparently mimic falling bombs after the war) and a manic monkey, housed in his own glass room. For the warmer months a Bedouin tent has been erected in front of the hotel and a Marsh-Arab reed hall is being constructed on the roof. The view over the Tigris from some of the rooms is fantastic. The food is generally good but the kebabs deserve a special recommendation. Parties are held most Thursdays, where for US$10 per head food is provided to the accompaniment of traditional music.

Security: Medium; benefits from some Sheraton/Palestine security

Rates: US$25–37 (normal) including breakfast and one main meal per day

D Hotel Atlas (45 rooms) Saadoun St, toward Tahrir Sq; tel: 717 2342/1984 or +472 4126200 [CC]. The rooms offer excellent value for money, are brightly painted, newly refurbished and each contains a satellite TV. The hotel also has a restaurant and a small shop. The only drawback is security. At the time of writing this end of Saadoun St is dangerous after dark, and uneasy even during the day. Avoid the rooms that face the road and do not walk outside at night; if you must leave after dark without your own transport ask reception to flag a taxi for you, and be vigilant even when driving. Check the current security advice, as this may change.

Security: Basic

Rates: US$35 (suite), US$15–25 (normal)

D Aghadir Hotel (100 rooms) Saadoun Street, toward the National Theatre [4 H6]. The rooms are basic and can look a little grubby at first sight, but they are cleaned daily and smell fresh. Reports from foreign guests are good.

Security: Low

Rates: US$30 (flat), US$15–20 (normal) including breakfast

D **Andalus Palace Hotel** (98 rooms) Saadoun St, toward the National Theatre [4 H6].
Small, very basic rooms that look slightly grimy, but do not smell musty and are regularly
cleaned. There is a laundry on the 8th floor, but no internet connection.

Security: Low

Rates: US$7–14 (normal) excluding breakfast, the price of the 3 to 5 bed suites is negotiable

Masbah/Karrada

Karrada (which takes its name from an old form of irrigation) is the bustling centre
of modern commerce, adjacent to Masbah, where most of the best restaurants are
found. Masbah literally means 'Swimming Pool' and there is a public pool by the river.

A **Baghdad Tower Hotel** (228 rooms) Area 904, St 17, Masbah; tel: +88 216 63225411
[4 J6]. All the rooms have heavy wooden furnishings, adding a certain grandeur even to the
smallest rooms – and the singles are small. The doubles are much larger, but many overlook
the main street. The suites at the back of the hotel sleep three and look on to a quiet
residential area. All rooms have satellite TV. The restaurant on the 9th floor has a stunning,
uninterrupted view of the bustling city below, which is particularly beautiful as the sun sets
and the buildings are transformed from a dusty beige to rose. A relatively (for Baghdad!)
large selection of alcohol is served.

Hotels

Security: Low
Rates: US$90 (suites),US$50–70 (normal)

$$$ Hamurabi Palace Hotel (60 rooms) al-Nidhal St, between the National Theatre and Aqba bin Nafi Sq; tel: 778 9556 or +88 216 88840636; email: Hamurabipalace3@hotmail.com. All of the rooms are spacious, bright and well furnished, and they all have satellite TV, receiving 16 channels, far more than the usual four or five. The de-luxe rooms are larger and contain a DVD player. The coffee shop and restaurant are well presented, the latter serving Western and Middle Eastern food and alcohol.

Security: Low, no roadblocks, but some security staff outside
Rates: US$70–100 (non-suite), US$100–130 (suite), includes breakfast, laundry and the use of the business centre.

B Rimal Hotel (58 rooms) Between Saadoun St and Nidhal St, the turning opposite the Hamurabi Palace Hotel; tel: +88 216 67745186; email: rimalhotel@warkaa.net or rimalhotel@hotmail.com [4 J6]. Although relatively small, this is one of the only hotels in Baghdad where the rooms could genuinely be compared to 'executive' rooms in Western cities. Bland and soulless can equally read comfortable and spanking clean. There is a small gym and sauna, business centre and restaurant. Don't get too worked up by the mention of a rooftop casino – it's an Arabian casino and as such provides little more excitement than a *nargileh* and a decent view.

Security: Medium, some road blocks and security measures
Rates: US$130–160 (normal), US$200 (suite), including breakfast

B Sebel Hotel (17 rooms) Masbah St, near German Embassy; tel: +88 216 67746104 [4 J6]. If you are looking for large, comfortable rooms the Sebel probably provides the best value for money. The rooms are extremely spacious with thick new carpets and equally new furniture, the bathrooms suites are gleaming and up to Western expectations. The owner is proud of the fact that he has the first hotel in Baghdad to operate a key-card system. Rooms have satellite TV and there is a small business centre. The only drawback is that there is no proper restaurant, only a café, and you cannot buy alcohol on the premises (although you are welcome to bring in your own supply). You are, however, in the heart of the restaurant quarter.

Security: Low, some basic security on the door

Rates: US$70 (single/double), US$100 (suite) including breakfast

C Janatadan Hotel (24 rooms) Arasat al-Hindiya; tel: 718 9734 or +88 216 2166 5242; email: hoteljanat@yahoo.com [4 H6]. Basic, clean rooms that are on the small side although doubles do have a small sitting-room. The furnishings are cheery and each has its own satellite. The hotel operates a pension system and does not serve food, but the location on Arasat means that most of the best restaurants in town are within a stone's throw. There is a meeting-room and small business centre.

Security: Low

Rates: US$50–75 (normal)

C Kandeel Hotel (24 rooms) al-Masbah Sq, opp al-Hindiya Club; tel: +88 216 5117 0108 [4 H6]. The suite is a small apartment with kitchen and relatively spacious sitting-room. The rooms are clean and well furnished if a little on the small side. All rooms have satellite connection. There is a business centre and a restaurant.

Hotels

Security: Low, some barriers outside the hotel
Rates: US$45–65 (normal), US$50–80 (suite)

C Orient Palace Hotel (44 rooms) Saadoun St, toward the German Embassy; tel: 719 60 41/44 fax: 719 6045; email: orpalace@hotmail.com [4 J6]. The suites are in good condition and include a dining table and kitchen making them better value than some apartments. The doubles and singles are of moderate size with basic furnishings, but they are clean, fresh and contain a satellite TV. The restaurant, *Fifties*, serves a good range of food and the cook is happy to make anything that isn't on the menu. Alcohol is served, with a bottle of wine costing around ID25,000.

Security: Low, there is a guard on the door
Rates: US$50–60 (suite), US$25–40 (normal), excluding breakfast

D al-Gader Hotel (86 rooms) Behind the National Theatre, opposite Orient Palace; tel: 718 2436 [4 H/J6]. Cheap, brightly decorated and cheerful and as a result highly popular with religious tourists. Iranian tour groups often block-book the entire hotel, so you may have difficulty getting a room for a length of time.

Security: Low
Rates: US$15 per person including three meals per day

D al-Masbah Palace Hotel (90 rooms) Saadoun St, diametrically opposite the German Embassy [4 H6]. While several foreign nationals stay here, at the time of writing there were no Western guests. All the rooms sleep two, so if you are staying on your own the rooms are spacious and good value. While the furnishings are basic, the rooms are clean and those on higher floors have a good view from the balcony. The internet café is open 24hr.

Security: Low
Rates: US$20 per person including breakfast, but you may be able to negotiate a discount if you share a room

Jadriya

In a tight loop of the river, leafy Jadriya is one of the more expensive residential areas of Baghdad, mingling among dense palm groves. Although beautiful, the time taken battling through Karrada during the rush hour should be considered. On the other hand, it provides the best access to Mansour. At the timeof writing, this has become the most popular area in which to live, with the focus on the Hamra.

A Babylon Hotel (260 rooms) Karrada-in, Jadriya; tel: 778 0029/8542/1964 or +88 216 5506035; fax: 717 1843 [4 F7]. Probably the nicest of the large hotels, the Babylon has a number of pluses; the communal areas lack the depressing boarding-school element that blights most of Baghdad's large hotels, the rooms are spacious and clean and the views in both directions are stunning. On the river side you are greeted by a wonderful vista of the Tigris with the Green Zone beyond, the skyline broken by the vast Jama al-Rahman (Mosque), the communications tower and the Zawra observation tower. On the other side the view encompasses the leafy palm groves of Jadriya. The atrium is filled with small shops selling everything from toothpaste and clothes to antiques. For the time being there is one bar and three restaurants (Chinese, French and the Coffee Shop). Facilities include four tennis courts, a billiard room, a basic gym, health suite and two large swimming pools. The indoor pool is heated and open year round (open 08.00–19.00, Tuesdays are for women only). The facilities are open to non-guests for a fee. As yet, the number of Western guests is far lower than in the Sheraton/Palestine complex, but it is popular with locals and regularly hosts wedding parties.

Security: Medium, the hotel is gated and set back from the road and Iraqi police man the gates
Rates: US$101 (suite), US$53-70 (normal)

A al-Hamra Hotel (190 rooms) Off Jamiya St, Jadriya; tel: 778 1805/6982; fax: 778 1806/7139; email: hamra_hotel_@yahoo.com or hamra@uruklink.net [4 F/G7]. The haunt of many journalists, the Hamra became the place to spend the hot summer evenings after the war, sipping beer around the pool, watching the sun set, and wondering whether this scene of Western decadence didn't present the perfect target. Like all the major hotels, it has had its scares, but has since significantly tightened up security. The rooms, spread over two towers, have satellite TV and are well presented and light, and the suites are particularly nice if you can afford them. There are two restaurants, one serving Chinese food, the other a selection of Western and Iraqi dishes, which can be eaten outside by the pool (a swim costs US$5 for non-guests). The pastry chief is well known in Baghdad and his creations are worth trying. The business centre opens 08.00–18.00.

Security: Medium, many of the surrounding streets have been blocked off and a blast wall has been erected around much of the hotel
Rates: US$90–130 (suite), US$70–90 (normal)

B Flower Land Hotel (31 rooms) Karrada-out, Jadriya, opposite the Hamra Hotel; tel: 776 26 03/02, 776 00 99/98; email: internet4u@hotmail.com (write to Abujan or Renna) [4

F/G7]. Rooms are well furnished and decorated, but can be a little small for the price. The hotel is popular nonetheless. The business centre is open 24hrs and the restaurant serves a variety of Western and Middle Eastern dishes. Satellite is available in rooms. There is a shop in the reception selling souvenirs.

Security: Medium, many of the roads have been closed off and there is a 24hr security guard by reception

Rates: US$91 (single), US$117 (double) including breakfast

C Karma Hotel (54 rooms) Jadriya St, near Hamra Hotel; tel: 778 6993/5314 [4 G7]. The doubles are the best rooms here, the suites having only a small, barely furnished sitting-room and a less spacious bedroom. The singles are very basic. There is a kitchen on each floor and a satellite TV in each room.

Security: Low

Rates: US$60–70 (suite), US$40–50 (normal) including breakfast

Elsewhere

A Mansour Melia Hotel (93 rooms refurbished, from total of 293) Haifa St, near Sinak Bridge [2 F4]. Ravaged by looting after the war, a photo display in the foyer shows burnt-out rooms, hanging cables and ruptured ceilings that makes the transition to its current state truly amazing. Echoing marble halls greet guests, but the rooms themselves are warm and bright. The bar is a particular highlight, if only because it boasts a cocktail menu and serves alcohol 24 hours. There is a restaurant, business centre, sauna, swimming-pool complex in the summer months and tennis courts. Once they have been redone, the gardens should be

Hotels

lovely. The Mansour is round the corner from the entrance to the Green Zone and Conference Centre.

Security: Medium, gated complex manned by Iraqi police, basic car checks for vehicles, but exposed

Rates: US$100-140 (normal), US$180 (suite)

APARTMENTS

If there are several of you or you're going to stay for a while, furnished, serviced apartments are a popular choice.

Saadoun area

al-Rabie Apartments (20 flats) St 45, off al-Saadoun St, opposite the Palestine Hotel; tel: 751 20 26/43; email: alnabhan23@yahoo.com [CC]. Well-presented one- or two-bedroom apartments (to sleep three or four), each with a basic kitchen (fridge, one-ring hob, sink and some utensils), sitting-room with satellite TV, and bathroom. Basic internet facilities.

Security: Medium; benefits from some Sheraton/Palestine security

Rates: US$40–50 per night

al-Andalus Apartments (30 flats) St 45, off al-Saadoun St, opposite the Palestine Hotel; tel/fax: 71 92303/84290; email: andalusp@yahoo.com [CC]. Spacious but Spartan best describes the al-Andalus apartments. Most have two bedrooms (to sleep four), a large sitting-room with satellite TV, bathroom and basic kitchen (fridge and sink, a stove can be negotiated). The communal area is very bright and cheery and the restaurant serves good food. Basic internet facilities.

Security: Medium; benefits from some Sheraton/Palestine security

Rates: US$50–60 per night

Masbah

B **Cedar Hotel** (30 flats) Opp Rimal Hotel; tel: +88 216 2155 0855 or 776 0707 [4 J6]. Not to be confused with the nearby al-Sidre Hotel, which now caters only for Iranian tour groups, the Cedar Hotel provides a range of spacious, clean and newly furnished apartments, all with satellite TV. The kitchens provide basic cooking facilities. There is a business centre, small gym, restaurant and a basement bar.

Security: Medium, some road blocks, a security guard on each floor at night

Rates: US$100–150 (for 1–2 people)

Jadriya

B **Sumer Land Hotel** (44 flats) Jadriya next to Karma Hotel; tel: 7787 135/596 778 2107; email: sumerlandik@hotmail.com or sumerlandik@yahoo.com [4 F/G7]. Almost every apartment is different so you should look at all the appropriate rooms on offer. Some are really very pleasant. Each flat has a kitchen with a stove, fridge and some utensils. The rooms are clean and all have decent furniture and satellite TV, while one wing has been newly decorated, unusually with furniture in keeping with Western taste. There is a tiny swimming pool for guests. The internet café is open 09.00–00.00, but a line can be taken up to the room. The Steak House restaurant serves as its name suggests, although there are a few other dishes on offer.

Security: Medium, benefits from some road closures and speed blocks
Rates: US$40–100+ per night with an additional US$10 per night for a stay under 2 weeks.

D Al-Dulaimi Apartments (30 flats) Jadriya, Quarter 913, St 10, near the Sumer Land Hotel; tel: 778 5150/0335 [4 F/G7]. The rooms can be very dark, and some smell musty. They vary both in size and style so look at what's on offer as the furnishings in a few may deeply offend those used to clean Scandinavian lines. There is satellite TV in the rooms and the kitchens have either a stove or a gas ring, utensils and a fridge. Good value for groups.
Security: Medium, benefits from some road closures and speed blocks
Rates: US$35–50 (to sleep 2–4)

D Al-Mosafer Apartments (18 flats) Jadriya, Quarter 913, St 10, near the Sumer Land Hotel; tel: 778 6738; fax: 778 0113 [4 F/G7]. The bedrooms are large if a little musty, and because they have all the external windows the sitting-rooms are rather dark. The kitchen contains a stove, fridge and some utensils. There is an internet-room downstairs.
Security: Medium, benefits from some road closures and speed blocks
Rates: US$40 (sleeps 4 people)

Eating and Drinking

5

Baghdadis love their food. Until the debilitating sanctions left most families with barely enough to feed themselves, Iraq was having to combat obesity. Even during the sanctions those rich enough or powerful enough (which was often the same thing) ensured they had a wide selection of delicacies at their disposal.

Masgouf is the most famous dish from Baghdad, but a number of other culinary delights await you. Quite apart from the wide selection of kebabs on offer, look out for the following.

For breakfast the local delicacy is *jemah (gemer)*, a sweet cream somewhere between crème-fraîche and thick whipped cream, eaten on bread with jam.

You don't really need to look out for *quzi*, as it will surely come to you if you stay long enough. A fragrant meat stew on rice, it can be made with any meat but on special occasions is prepared with saddle of lamb. *Barmia* is similar but made with okra.

All Baghdad's ethnic groups enjoy *kubba*, although each has their own specialities. As Claudia Roden says in *The Book of Jewish Cooking*, 'You could call them dumplings, but they are a many-splendoured thing that defies characterisation.' *Kubba* is basically minced meat encased in a shell, usually made from cracked wheat or rice flour. Most fall into two main categories, dry *kubba* and wet *kubba*. The former, often fried, is either served on its own (as in the pancake-flat Mosul *kubba*) or with a delicious mixture of fried vegetables. Wet kubba is firmer and floats in a variety of rich, tasty sauces.

MASGOUF

No trip to Baghdad is complete without sampling masgouf. Universally enjoyed by Baghdadis it is even rumoured that on a state visit to France Saddam Hussein travelled with a supply of the appropriate Tigris fish and ordered his bemused French chiefs to cook him masgouf. It is even said that Jacques Chirac developed a taste for it.

Masgouf is not actually a type of fish but the manner in which it is cooked. The word masgouf comes from the Iraqi word sakff, which means roof. Traditionally the wood from the fire used to cook the fish also formed a partial roof around the fish to heat it from all sides. This method is no longer employed among the street fish sellers. Nonetheless watching the masgouf being prepared is fascinating.

Karrada-in is lined with the huge polystyrene tanks filled with flapping fish, from which you select your carp. It is then de-scaled, gutted and opened up

If you're not afraid of deep-fried food then *greem chap* is delicious. Herbed minced lamb is surrounded in spicy mashed potato and fried into a crisp patty. *Dolme* are vegetables stuffed with rice and meat. Although peppers are the most usual, aubergines, potatoes and onions are also used. Onion *dolme* is especially popular and can be bought mixed with stuffed vine leaves.

from the back until it looks like a flatfish. This is then attached to small wooden stakes and placed on a brazier, about 30cm from a smoky fire traditionally made of wood from the Tarfa tree. After 30mins of gentle smoking and cooking the fish is removed from the stakes closed and placed in the ashes around the fire until the skin is brown. The masgouf is then packed in flat bread and whisked home to be eaten hot with onions and tomatoes.

Traditionally, the fishermen would sell and cook their catch along the riverbank. The fish were kept fresh in the hot weather by tethering them with long strings and returning them to the Tigris. Unfortunately the famous masgouf restaurants along Abu Newas Street are now closed, but a few remain in Jadriya.

The traditional dish for large parties is *glamiya*. A semi-flat bread is covered in a rich aromatic broth then smothered with a thick layer of rice and finally topped with chunks of barbecued meat. Also found on special occasions is the famous *pacha*, or sheep's head. If you want to try it, the open-air eateries down Abu Nidhal Street used to be famous for *pacha* and *sujuk*, the local haggis-cum-sausage.

Eating and drinking

Appetizers, while plentiful, have their disappointments. *Hummus* in Baghdad bears little resemblance to the Mediterranean version and the *fatoush*, a salad with croutons and balsamic vinegar, does not live up to its Lebanese cousin. But Baghdad also has its successes. *Babaganooj* is delectable if you are an aubergine lover. Unlike the version available in Jordan and Lebanon it consists of a paste rather than chunks. The predominant flavour is of smoked aubergine, but puréed lamb adds taste as well as texture. Most are astounded to discover that it isn't vegetarian, so don't expect the added lamb to give a meaty taste.

Several types of bread are available in Baghdad, but the most common (outside Western hotels where they often assume foreigners prefer slightly stale white rolls) is *samoon*, lozenge-shaped leaven bread with a cavity inside. These are delicious when still warm from the brick oven but become rapidly inedible, turning into a potential weapon within a couple of hours. There are two types of flat bread: one can be stuffed, the other is used as a wrap.

While the prevalence of kebabs and meat-based stews can make eating hard for committed **vegetarians,** options are available. Once you have got over the initial battle to persuade those cooking for you that a chicken really isn't a vegetable, you should be fine. **Vegans** in Baghdad may face more of an uphill battle; make sure you bring a translation of your vegan passport. Even armed with that it may be several days before the disbelief in vegetarians who won't eat omelette subsides. Once you've got the message across and worked out what to ask for when eating away from your usual haunt, you should be fine.

For vegetarians and vegans *fasolia* or *yabse*, the local form of beans in tomato sauce, is a good option although you will have to ask that meat stock not be used in the sauce. The meat can similarly be taken out of *quzi* and *barmia*. Falafels are good, if a little greasy, and available piping hot from street-sellers. Most appetizers are fine, but be aware that Iraqi *babaganooj* contains lamb.

For a bustling family atmosphere and a window into local life take an early evening trip down **al-Rubayee Street**. At the end of the road is a children's funfair that opens at dusk and the street is lined with street-sellers hawking their wares from dimly lit stalls. Here also are fast-food joints, juice bars and ice-cream parlours that come alive in a myriad dancing neon lights as whole families step out after dark to promenade and squabble over mountainous, luminous ices. The ice cream is surprisingly good, but only for those prepared to ingest a cocktail of E-numbers.

For those in need of more healthy refreshment, two of the best juice bars in town are at either end of the street, **Sandra Juice** and **Laymona**. The 'fruit cocktail' from Sandra Juice, a blend of peach, strawberry, banana, lemon and chocolate, is worth a trip in itself. The summer months turn Sandra Juice into something of a pilgrimage site for thirsty foreign freelancers.

Women are not allowed inside the *nargileh* and coffee shops that line the street, but both are reputed to be good. Most have tables outside where women are allowed.

Drinking alcohol is still something only to be done in Western restaurants and hotels. There has been a rise in the number of vigilantes so don't linger around alcohol shops or local watering-holes. Stick to well-known brands of spirits: the cheap replicas are a one-way ticket to the worst hangover of your life. Cans of pre-mixed gin and tonic and cherry vodka are particularly lethal. If you drink spirits in the summer make sure you compensate by drinking sufficient water as you may already be dehydrated from sweating.

Beer was first invented in Iraq and until sanctions slowed down production there were several 'large' breweries (defined as producing over 1 million barrels of beer per year) producing the best pint in the region. The breweries came under close scrutiny by UN weapons inspectors, intent on insuring they weren't being used to brew something more lethal than beer. There is still some local beer being produced, despite a number of attacks by hardliners, but there are concerns about the purity of the water used. Arak is distilled locally, with the typical taste of aniseed. Some bottles on sale look as though they should be avoided. For oenophiles new to the region, Lebanese reds can be exceptional and price-for price usually provide the best value.

RESTAURANTS

Prepare to discover a surprising restaurant culture in Baghdad, particularly given the years of otherwise crippling sanctions. Since the fall of the previous regime restaurants have been reopening and renovating, hoping to cash in on the complete dearth of evening activities; going to a restaurant is likely to remain the highlight of any night out in Baghdad for some time, whenever the security situation permits.

The biggest problem with restaurants in Baghdad is the lack of consistency. A restaurant that produces exquisite food on one trip may well bitterly disappoint the next time you visit.

Tragically the Cassandras were proved correct on New Year's eve when Nabil's, a long-time favourite with foreigners, was the target of a deadly car bomb. At least eight people were killed and many more wounded. There is no doubt that many of the best restaurants provide soft targets for terrorists, particularly those regularly frequented by foreigners. The best advice is to sit as far away from windows and the road as possible. Eat at home when kidnapping remains a threat.

While there are only a few restaurants that serve good Western food, Baghdad is full of excellent restaurants offering traditional cuisine. They may have neon signs and plastic tables adorned with a fake red rose, but the food will make up for the lack of ambience. Ask your translator to recommend some that he thinks will be safe to eat in.

Before the war Abu Newas Street was famous for its fish. Lined with open-air restaurants, this was where Baghdad's famous fish dish, the *masgouf,* would be barbecued in front of hungry diners enjoying the cool river breezes. These are now all closed, but a few similar restaurants remain in Jadriya.

Many hotels have good restaurants, particularly the smaller, more intimate, hotels such as al-Finar, the Orient Palace, and the Sumer Land.

What follows are some of the better restaurants in Baghdad, but there are many more. Bear in mind that although they are good, we're not in the world of *Michelin* stars.

ARASAT AL-HINDIYA
(SKETCH MAP)

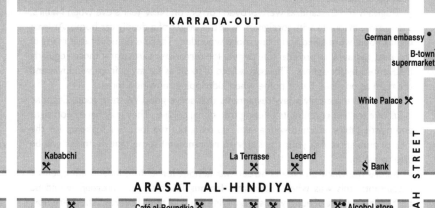

Serwan Alcohol store

N
Bradt

KARRADA-OUT

German embassy

B-town supermarket

White Palace

STREET

Kababchi

La Terrasse

Legend

$ Bank

ARASAT AL-HINDIYA

Café al-Boundkia

al-Lathiqia

Qamar al-Zaman

Golden Fingers
Alcohol store

MASBAH

Babeesh Grill

Pizza Reef
Coral Beach

© Bradt Travel Guides Ltd

Non-Iraqi cuisine

Babeesh Grill Restaurant Bottom of Arasat al-Hindiya on the left; tel: 778 4457 [map opposite]. If you can ever decide what to order from the bewildering array on offer, you will not be disappointed. From chicken kievs oozing with garlic butter to traditional Iraqi kebabs, the food here is excellent and by encompassing both Western and Arabian dishes the menu caters for all tastes. There is a large selection of fish and seafood and if you order in advance they can even rustle up a stuffed goose. Although less cosy than Pizza Reef, Babeesh achieves a more sophisticated atmosphere, the only flaw being the tinned music that is at least unobtrusive. The waiters are exceptionally attentive, so much so that smokers may find the ashtray removed and replaced twice in the space of one cigarette. Alcohol is served, with a bottle of wine starting at around US$20.

Price: Most main courses are around US$7 although some are much higher; starters are around US$4

Open 12.00–16.00, 19.00–23.00

La Coquette al-Nidhal St, opposite Hamurabi Palace Hotel; tel: +88 216 3331 0366 or 717 3003 [4 J6]. The Tunisian owner and chef, Oncle Ben, is exceptionally obliging, eager to please, and moreover speaks fluent French and some English. His genuine concern for his guests makes eating here a much more personal affair than is usual in Baghdad. There are a small number of Tunisian dishes available on a separate menu that are highly recommended, but the body of the menu is French. The appetizers are particularly good, especially the pâté and the Spanish omelette although if you don't mind mixing cultures the *babaganooj* is exceptional. The sauces served are well made, but be aware generally that should you order

Restaurants

steak the larger cuts available in Baghdad are not particularly suited to Western dishes and if unlucky you may end up feeling like Charlie Chaplin eating his boots. The restaurant is happy to host large parties (holding up to 200 people if required) and there is live music and oriental dancing on Tuesdays, Thursdays and Saturdays.

Price: Around US$10 for starter and main course, bottle of wine US$20
Open 12.00–00.00

Coral Beach Restaurant Off Arasat al-Hindiya, opposite Pizza Reef; tel: 718 2711/8049 [map page 140]. This is Baghdad's answer to the bistro: 1920s' poster art, a multitude of nautical knick-knacks, muted lighting, and with a jazz and blues accompaniment mumbling in the background, it is all too easy to forget where you are. The food fits the mood with a wide selection of excellent bistro fare. The prawn cocktail deserves a mention, although Iraqi appetisers are also worth ordering. The lamb chops are quite exceptional, tender and fragrant and the other meats are well served and succulent. The only warning goes on the chicken cordon bleu, in which bacon is replaced by chicken spam, but if you've developed a taste for Baghdad's 'mortadella' then you'll have no other complaints. Service is good, and the series of alcoves mean that you can establish your own corner.

Price: Around US$10 for starter and main course; bottle of wine starts at ID30,000
Open 10.00–00.00

Legend Restaurant Halfway down Arasat al-Hindiya on the right; tel: 718 6729 [map page 140]. The assortment of Chinese paraphernalia, in particular the heavy carved chairs, are probably the most interesting thing about this restaurant. The noodles are good, but the main dishes got lost somewhere between China and Iraq. It provides a good change from the usual fare, especially if you like duck, but don't expect anything too authentic. The restaurant does not serve alcohol, but if you ask you can bring in your own supply.

Price: Around US$7 per head

Open 12.00–22.00

Pizza (Cafeteria al-Boundkia) Bottom Arasat al-Hindiya on the left; tel: 718 7828 [map page 140]. Small and cheerful with additional seating outside, the food here is both tasty and inexpensive. The variety of pizza is limited but all are good, with a thin base and lots of cheese. They also serve a number of pasta dishes and Arabian starters.

Price: Around US$2 for a pizza

Open 11.00–14.00 and 17.00–22.00

Pizza Reef Restaurant 9th St off Arasat al-Hindiya, if counting while coming from Masbah (visible from Arasat) [map page 140]. Certainly one of the best Western restaurants in Baghdad, come here to escape from it all and pretend you are back at home. Candlelight, crisp white tablecloths and good service complement the wide range of excellent Italian food. The experience is further enhanced by imaginative presentation, from salads in edible bowls to moulded spaghetti dishes. While Western cheese is not Baghdad's strong point, there are several used here and mercifully no sign of the ubiquitous tinned cheddar. Wine is served year round, the Lebanese reds being particularly good. The only word of caution goes to traditional pizza lovers who should make sure they ask for a thin base.

Price: Main courses are priced around US$5, starters US$2; wine starts from around US$15 per bottle

Open 12.00–00.00

Restaurants

Ramaya Masbah St, between streets 14 and 15; tel: 717 82 98/99 [4 H/J7]. Excellent food and a sophisticated atmosphere easily make this one of the best restaurants in Baghdad. In the spring and summer the terrace is opened for Mediterranean grills and Lebanese mezze. The à la carte has an Italian bias, and the steaks and escalopes are delicious, although the former are not offered rare. While the chief would probably be mortified to discover people coming solely for the chips, it is one of the only places in town where they are neither soggy nor made with sugary potatoes. The garlic bread with cheese has gained some renown, and the salads provide interesting innovations on otherwise mundane staples. Alcohol is served with wine starting at US$10 per bottle.

Price: Around US$10 per head without alcohol

Open 12.00–00.00, last orders 22.00

Saj al-Reef St 62, Masbah [4 J6]. Once you have had lunch here, it will be hard to go elsewhere. The list of 'must try' foods is almost as long as the menu, but a special mention must be made of the *mana'eesh*, a Lebanese pizza topped with thyme, and the *saj*, a range of delicious wraps. The translucently thin and elastic flatbread is as fascinating for its texture as its taste. Although they do take-aways the log tables and benches provide a pleasant lunchtime atmosphere. At night, however, it can get unpleasantly crowded and the waiters are rushed off their feet. Service at all other times is quick and functional.

Price: Lunch costs around ID4,000, dinner with starters around ID6,000

Open 10.00–22.00

La Terrasse Arasat al-Hindiya above M clothing store [map page 140]. The space-age tinted blue windows, funky bar and fibre-optic star-scape may be naff, but it's as near as you're going to get to trendy in Baghdad. The upstairs town-centre location, open-plan dining area and single entrance (making security searches easier) makes this a great location for a party. Sadly, the food does not quite live up to the promisingly different décor. The Western, Middle Eastern and Chinese meals available are all perfectly acceptable but none leaps on to the taste buds, and there are equally pleasant if less avant-garde restaurants that serve better food for an equivalent price.

Price: Around US$10 for starter and main course; wine starts at US$15 a bottle
Open 12.00–10.00

Middle Eastern cuisine

al-Gouta Restaurant Off Saadoun St, near Kahramana Sq; tel: 718 4972 [4 H5]. A large, cheerful restaurant with a delightful garden in the summer, al-Gouta is deservedly popular with Iraqis. Although there is a Western menu, the large selection of kebabs makes Iraqi cuisine the obvious choice. Meals are served with an alarmingly large selection of starters which, aided by the fact that they are all delicious, means you must be careful not to lose your appetite before the equally gargantuan main course arrives. Make sure you ask for *antabli* if you order kebab: a spicy vegetable ragout sandwiched between two pieces of flatbread and flame-grilled with the meat. Smoking an apple *nargileh* provides a perfect end to the evening.

Price: around ID10,000 for starters, main course and soft drinks
Open 09.00–23.00

Kababchi Bottom Arasat al-Hindiya on the right [map page 140]. Kababchi used to be one of the best-known restaurants in Baghdad, vying with Babeesh across the street. There is now a

marked difference between the two, but Kababchi is still worth a visit. There is a small selection of Western food but the emphasis is on Arabian cuisine catering for Iraqi tastes. As a result, conservative foreigners might find the flavours slightly unusual; the appetizers include the pickles and bitter yoghurt dressings found in Iraqi home cooking and the lamb dishes have the distinctive overtone of mutton. This should not put you off, however, as the food is well prepared and includes some interesting alternatives to the usual kebab. *Arayees* is certainly worth a try. Originally eaten in Syria and Lebanon, it lies somewhere between a pie and a toasty with a spiced lamb filling. If you find it too greasy, place it between two slices of flatbread to absorb the excess oil. In the summer the veranda windows are opened and the front half of the restaurant becomes open air. Alcohol is served, with wine starting at around US$7 per bottle.
Price: Around US$5 for main course, standard appetizers and soft drink
Open 12.00–00.00

Khan Mirjan Near Central Bank, Shorjah [CC]. Originally built in 1359 as a hotel for merchants, Khan Mirjan has been converted into an up-market restaurant once fabled for nightly performances of traditional music, usually performed by the best groups in Iraq. Unfortunately, the security situation has put an end to that and the area in which it is located is deserted after dark. The restaurant still serves lunch, and the beauty of the building is untouched, making it an imposing place in which to eat. Once inside, you escape the crush of the surrounding market streets, but take care when getting there.
Open 09.00–16.00

al-Lathiqia Restaurant Halfway down Arasat al-Hindiya on the left; tel: 719 7084 or +88 216 5551 9305 [map page 140]. This is the place for kebab-lovers growing tired of the usual

selection. From well-spiced tikkas to the scented 'kebab with aubergine', there is a kebab here for all tastes although without Arabic it can be hard to establish exactly what you've ordered. The portions are huge so you'll need to be exceptionally hungry to do them justice. Meals are served with a good selection of appetizers and sesame flatbread. The waiters are friendly, some speak English and the atmosphere is bright and airy, and enhanced by an indoor fountain.
Price: Around US$6 per head including fresh juice and coffee
Open 08.00–00.00

Mahabar Restaurant Salman Faiq [4 H6]. Serves a good selection of Iraqi food and a number of Western staples. Food comes with the usual range of side dishes. The staff are friendly, but communication can be a problem if you don't speak Arabic. The eatery nextdoor makes delicious fresh patties and local pizzas, perfect for a take-away lunch, particularly when complemented by salads and dips from the Mahabar.
Price: Around ID5,000 per head, for main course, soft drink and appetizers
Open 12.00–21.30

Qamar al-Zaman Restaurant Arasat al-Hindiya; tel: +88 216 2123 8902 [map page 140]. Newly refurbished, this is a restaurant favoured by the Iraqi élite. The décor is sultry with a series of alcoves giving some privacy from other diners. Live piano music adds a touch of the palm court, and a reprieve from the universally annoying canned music so often found. The food is good, particularly the mixed grill, and the staff obliging.
Price: Around ID20,000 per head for main course and starters; a bottle of wine about ID30,000
Open 12.00–00.00

White Palace Masbah St, opposite the German Embassy [map page 140]. Serving a large variety of Iraqi and European cuisine, the White Palace specialises in hearty, wholesome food – and lots of it. The service is good and the waiters are happy to make recommendations if the selection and amusing mistranslations leave you unable to choose. The atmosphere is bright, functional and clean. Exceptionally inexpensive for what it offers, this is a great place for anyone on a budget.

Price: Around ID5,000 per head, for main course, soft drink and appetizers
Open 12.00–21.30

Other restaurants to try include
Corner Arasat al-Hindiya
Al-Finjan 72 St, al-Wahda district
Sayseban Karrada, out near the Hamra Hotel
Sa'ah Mansour. Famous for being the restaurant in which Saddam was eating when a US missile struck nearby houses. Different food is served depending on whether you dine upstairs or downstairs.
Abu Jalal Near the German Embassy. Recommended for take-aways.
Serwan Grill Off Saadoun St opposite the al-Masbah Palace Hotel. A small kebab joint which serves basic but tasty kebabs. Also features a singing canary.

Entertainment and Nightlife

6

What to do with your free time can be one of the biggest drawbacks to life in Baghdad, particularly if you find yourself at a loose end in the evening. At the moment there are no nightclubs, except for the weekly Thursday-night disco in the al-Rasheed basement. But attractive as that prospect may seem after a few weeks in the city, to get in you either have to live in the Green Zone or have someone willing to sign you in.

There are a number of bars in hotels around town. The Cedar, the Mansour and the Babylon all have bars that aspire to be something more than an extension of the hotel lobby. The bar at the top of the Baghdad Tower Hotel has a fantastic view, although in reality it is merely part of the restaurant. At the time of writing the newly opened restaurant/bar at the al-Finar throws weekly parties with traditional food and music for a US$10 entrance fee. Alcohol is extra but there is a wide selection.

In the summer, hotel swimming pools become the focus of expat life. In the months after the war the Hamra Hotel was the place to go as people clustered round the pool to cool off, relax, enjoy the tinned music and network.

Although theatres are reopening the performances have all been in Arabic, but it is certainly worth dropping round to see if this has changed. There are no concert halls in Baghdad; the former home of the Iraqi Symphony Orchestra is now in the internationally controlled Conference Centre.

Right now cinemas are no-go areas for Westerners, especially women. The only films showing are 'blue', many relatively hardcore. Pragmatic owners see this as a way

BAGHDAD RACETRACK

The new track was only opened in 1993 (after Saddam requisitioned the previous track in the heart of Mansour in order to build the al-Rahman Mosque), and still remains a riot of half completed buildings, the twisting iron supports clamouring against each other in the hot gusts of air. While the members' section has been completed, punters are left to withstand the whirling dust and sunlight perched on two racks of splintering wooden terraces.

In the summer the shimmering heat is intolerable. As the starting bell sounds for the first race of the day the red line on the club's thermometer edges towards 50 degrees centigrade. The nimbus of dust surrounding the horses rushes nearer until they streak past, a blur of colour in the otherwise monochrome landscape. Normally the season ends in June and only recommences in the autumn, the races held in the relative cool of the evenings. But in the current situation no one would come after dark and many owners are so short of money (punters are down by about 80%) that officials are

of making money in a city where families are too nervous to go out en masse. Cinemas have also become clandestine gay meeting points, increasing the risk of possible attack.

It is certainly worth bringing a computer that plays DVDs and a good supply of films. Stalls selling pirated films in CD format abound; all the very latest compelled to extend the season. This takes its toll on the horses; a number have had to leave races suffering from heat-related complaints.

Although Iraq was once one of the breeding centres of pure Arab horses, most are now a nondescript mixture. Traditionally the club had a strict arab-only policy, until Uday Hussein insisted that the rules be changed to allow him to race his foreign horses. With arabs unable to compete with fleet European breeds over shorter distances and owners forbidden to import their own thoroughbreds, a gradual process of mixing began.

Although the club is now free of Uday's grip and jockeys can loose without fear of being beaten, his legacy continues. The club's assets have been frozen and the race-track is in sore need of money to complete the buildings and hire professional foreign trainers.

The race-track is a microcosm of its city – there is an overwhelming desire to consign the past and its degeneracy to history and to focus on an international future, as soon as there is money and stability to do so.

blockbusters are available for a couple of dollars, but the quality is atrocious and they have a nasty habit of crashing irrevocably a few minutes before the final climax.

Gyms abound in Baghdad and Iraq has produced several great weightlifting champions of the past. Many have women-only days, but foreigners of either sex

SPORT IN BAGHDAD
Seb Walker

Iraqis are obsessed with sport. They take great pride in the fact that the national soccer team was widely regarded in the seventies and eighties as the best among the Gulf countries. Sadly, when Saddam's notoriously brutal eldest son, Uday, decided to get involved with the running of the national team, things started to go horribly wrong.

Uday's prime motivational tactic was to make his players afraid of losing. According to professional Iraqi footballers unlucky enough to play under Uday, bad performances were punished with jail terms, and sometimes physical torture. This did not make for success on the pitch and ultimately caused Iraq to be banned from international competition by Fifa (football's governing body).

The Iraq national team is now back and showing much of the talent for which the country was once renowned

After soccer, the second national sporting obsession is bodybuilding. All around Baghdad you can spot drawings of semi-naked men with cartoon physiques, which indicate a gymnasium dedicated to maintaining the body beautiful.

will be met with intense curiosity and it is probably best sticking to hotel gyms despite their limited facilities.

Inside, men with huge muscles pump iron to the accompaniment of deafening heavy metal music. This is not just an exercise in vanity – bodybuilding is a serious sport for many Iraqis who dream of becoming professional and partaking in international competitions.

In 1972, the world bodybuilding championships were held in Baghdad and an Iraqi called Ali Al-Gayah managed to carry off the bronze medal, beating Arnold Schwarzenegger into fourth place. But, more recently, life has been difficult for professional Iraqi bodybuilders.

Under sanctions, it was hard to get hold of vital supplies like protein supplements or even a sufficiently nutritious diet. Furthermore, this sport too was taken over by Uday, which made bodybuilders understandably reluctant to remain involved.

With the fall of the ex-regime, athletes from across the spectrum of Iraqi sport were hopeful that there would be a rejuvenation of the country's sports facilities and organisations. At time of writing, however, Iraqis have enough problems maintaining basic security and public services in their country before they can concentrate on restoring Iraqi sport to its once-proud position.

All of the larger hotels have health suites, and non-guests can attend for a fee. They are limited to extremely basic weights equipment, ageing treadmills and bicycles and the odd mossy-looking sauna. Outdoor swimming is confined to the six hot months of the year, but the Babylon Hotel has a large, heated indoor pool that remains open all year round. Several of the larger hotels have tennis courts.

One of the few sources of entertainment remaining is the racetrack, which runs races every Friday in season. US forces have taken over a part of the grounds, affording additional protection and an initial checkpoint. A far cry from anything you will have experienced in the West, it is nonetheless a fun day out and the organisers are extremely friendly. If you enjoy riding then it is worth chatting to some of the owners in the VIP lounge; several of them are in the process of setting up riding schools.

For a more intellectual pass-time, why not learn Arabic? Several language schools are in the process of starting up, although it may be some months before they open. The best way to find a teacher is by word of mouth, so ask around. Prices usually range from US$5 to US$25 per hour depending on teaching experience and English ability.

The French Cultural Centre on Abu Newas used to run courses, concerts and exhibitions. It intends to open again as soon as the situation permits, but that may be some time yet.

THEATRES

National Theatre Between Saadoun St and Nidhal St, on Fateh Sq. The beautiful National Theatre is one of the landmarks of central Baghdad. Open once again, painted banners usually advertise what's playing, but it's worth squeezing in through one of the bricked-off doors to speak to someone inside.

al-Rasheed Theatre Haifa St, opposite the Meilia Mansour Hotel. Although the stage and seating remain unscathed it will be some time before the theatre recovers from devastating post-war fires and looting.

Abu Newas Theatre Abu Newas, next to the river and opposite Dijla Art Gallery

OTHER ENTERTAINMENT
Auction House [1 E2]
87 al-Imam al-A'adham St, al-Adhamiya; tel: +88 216 7744 5852; email: dr.t@antiquescity.net

Every other Friday, the 'Christies of Baghdad' holds an antiques auction. While the items going under the hammer may not be quite up to those put forward by its illustrious namesake, there are some interesting pieces on offer. Before the war there were different categories of auction, but now everything from suites of furniture to antique carpets are all bundled together. The auction house is open for viewing from 10.00 to 14.00. With many items, if the starting price has no bid the price will be lowered until bidding begins, which increases the chance of picking up a bargain. The general manager, Mokdad al-Baghdadi, is well informed and will tell you about the items on display. At the moment auctions are being held at 11.00, but check in advance.

Zawra Park [3 E5]
A visit to the **zoological gardens**, set in the heart of Zawra Park, can be either a surreal or a disturbing experience, depending on your concern for animal welfare.

Other entertainment

Most of the animals disappeared after the fall of Baghdad and the empty cages are filled with dogs of every shape and size. The addition of a couple of pedigree lapdogs only heightens the impression of having dropped by a landscaped dogs' home. A few of the original animals remain, with several big cats, brown bears, ostriches, a badger and a wild boar being the highlights, but most look bored and jolly miserable. As long as you can stand this, the zoo and surrounding park is a pleasant place to spend a few leisurely hours thanks to a massive clean-up operation lead by the Australian Army.

The water and trees provide an additional lure in the hot summer months. Several stalls sell refreshments and food and there are a number of picnic benches and playgrounds. At the moment the **planetarium**, located in the corner of the park nearest to the zoo, has been taken over for use as the Ministry of Youth and Sport. The **funfair**, close to the main entrance, is probably best avoided.

Art galleries

There is now no central art gallery in Baghdad after looting and fire obliterated almost the entire collection of the **Saddam Art Centre**, on Haifa Street. Although restoration work has begun, it will not be open for some time. Some artists, fearing a similar fate for their works, have withdrawn them from the remaining private galleries, preferring to sell directly out of their studios.

Despite such problems, the small galleries are worth a visit if only to see that art in Baghdad is thriving. From time to time they put on special exhibitions.

All the galleries sell the works displayed and the prices are low, canvasses by well-known Iraqi artists can be bought for under US$500. If you are interested in buying, most galleries have additional storerooms in which to browse. More representational paintings can be bought in hotel foyers and in shops along Karrada-in.

The following list is not comprehensive and does not include private studios.

Galleries in affluent Wazeriya, the old heartland of the ministerial class who gave the area its name, are all within a few minutes of the well-known **College of Fine Arts**. Once there, people will point you in the right direction. For those interested in painting, this is a good area in which to buy materials.

Hewar Art Gallery Near Turkish embassy; tel/fax: 425 0086; tel: +88 216 2183 0026; email: hewar@warkaa.net. Owned by Qasim al-Sabti the gallery has a permanent collection, but this is only open when he is present, so check before arriving. The works for sale are predominantly modern and include paintings and small sculpts. The gallery has a charming courtyard in which tea and sandwiches are served, and poets, artists and musicians gather to converse. The hum of voices unstrained by traffic noise and a leafy garden populated with sculptures, make this a place in which to escape. *Open 09.00–17.00.*

Athar Art Gallery Behind the college of Fine Arts; tel: 422 8957; email: mznad@hotmail.com. Two minutes away from Hewar, the Athar Gallery sells a similar selection of modern paintings and sculptures. *Open 10.00–14.00, 18.00–20.00.*

Other entertainment

Al-Rewaq Gallery Maghreb St; tel/fax: 425 8293; email: rewaq@warkaa.net. With a smaller display than the other galleries in the area, it is marked out by being naturally well lit, important at a time when power cuts are still frequent. *Open 09.00–17.00.*

Private Museum Two houses away from Athar Art Gallery; email: mznad@hotmail.com. As yet unnamed, this is the brainchild of Mohammed Znad, owner of the Athar Art Gallery. With French backing, he is well on the way to completing the building in which he hopes to house a permanent retrospective of Iraqi art over the last 100 years. His personal collection of 800 pieces, representing all the major Iraqi artists of the last century, will form the body of the museum. With the looting of the Saddam Art Centre, this will in all likelihood be the only place to provide an overview of art in Iraq in the foreseeable future. A complete catalogue should be available. It is hoped to be open by winter 2004.

Abu Newas Street boasts another cluster of art galleries, all within walking distance from the Palestine/Sheraton complex.

Inaa Art Gallery 53 Abu Newas St; tel: 718 7836. Right next door to the al-Finar Hotel, the gallery has a good selection of watercolours and wooden sculptures as well as selling ceramics and modern paintings. *Open 09.00–21.00.*

Akkad Art Gallery 77 Abu Newas St; tel: 717 5504/719 7612. Three minutes' walk from the Inaa Gallery, the gallery covers three floors and has a wide variety of paintings and sculptures. The third floor is dedicated to realism. *Open 09.00–17.00.*

Dijla Gallery Abu Newas, near the French Cultural Centre. *Open 10.00–14.00, 16.00–21.00.*

Shadad Gallery Off Abu Newas, one street in from the al-Finar. *Open 10.00–14.00.*

Sports clubs
Baghdad Equestrian Club
Highway One, al-Amriya near Abu Graib

Races are held at midday on Sunday, Wednesday and Friday. The day ends at about 17.30 in the summer and provides a fun day out. The only legal form of betting is on the club's tote system where the returns are low. Unless you can gain access to the VIP lounge, less plush than it's name suggests, then prepare to spend a hot and tiring day. The stands are in the sun and the covered section has no seating. Women are allowed, but you will almost certainly be the only one there.

al-Alwiya Club [4 H5]
Firdos Square, next to the Sheraton

The al-Alwiya Club is a hangover from the days of kings and mandates. Its grandeur is so faded it is almost forgotten, but the staff are very pleasant and the facilities good. There is a members' bar (dark wood, cabinets full of silver and a faintly seedy air), a large billiard room, a swimming pool, restaurants and numerous tennis courts.

Tennis lessons are inexpensive and they will find you a partner if you can't find your own. For the more enthusiastic there are various ladders and organised matches.

On public holidays the al-Alwiya heaves with Baghdad's professional classes, the adults sip cola under leafy arbours while carefully dressed young men and women promenade around the gardens in strictly segregated couples. Membership currently costs only around US$20 per month.

Other entertainment

Boat trip

Many of the old Ottoman houses that border the Tigris can be appreciated only from the river. The beautiful building that used to house the British Embassy is one such.

Small motor-powered boats chug backward and forward from near the Central Bank to the base of Shuhada Bridge. For a few dollars and a few minutes' bargaining the boat and boatman can become yours for an hour. Travelling up to Adhamiya, the Ottoman Palace and Abbasid Palace are on your left. Further up, the white mansion raised on the banks of the river is the Sassoon Palace. On your return, there is a brilliant opportunity to photograph the river borders and minarets of Old Baghdad.

Travelling towards Jumhuriya Bridge, notice the Ottoman buildings on both sides of the river, glorious in their decay.

While it may be tempting to go further downstream there is little to see and the close proximity to the Presidential Palace and the Green Zone will almost certainly see your peace destroyed by low-flying helicopters trying to ascertain whether you pose a threat.

The best time of day to take a trip is just before sunset, but you will need to arrange this in advance. You should aim to leave while the last yellow rays of the sun beat down on the walls of Mustansiriya and the palaces, when they are at their best, the dying light turning them ochre and then pink. The sunset from the boat is magical, but make sure you are returned to a waiting car well before dusk.

Shopping

7

Arriving in Baghdad for the first time, it can come as a surprise to find a booming commodities market. Business is thriving, particularly for electronic goods and the consequent increase in electricity consumption is cited as a major factor in the continued power shortfall. Optimistic shop owners can even be seen peddling electric radiators in the height of the gruelling summer months.

Most electronic goods are therefore available in Baghdad, and visitors need not arrive burdened down with alarm clocks, radios and torches, although for those spending large amounts of time outside the city it's worth importing something reliable.

New supermarkets are opening around Baghdad and a wider range of Western food can now be purchased, though often at inflated prices. Corner shops abound and sell staple goods, including bottled water, tinned food, sweets and biscuits. All the large hotels have small shops in the foyer selling essentials at exorbitant prices. For those with the facilities to cook seriously, the best food is available from specialist shops. There are no shortages of fruit and vegetable stalls, butchers, dairy shops and bakeries. Fruit and vegetables are usually cheap enough to make bargaining unnecessary, but when buying meat it is worth asking an Iraqi for help in negotiating a fair price. Meat in Iraq is good, the lamb is particularly tender, although there may be difficulty explaining what cut is required.

Availability of fruit and vegetables is completely seasonal, but every season has its delights. Particularly look out for pomegranates and dates in the early autumn, peaches and apricots in the spring and figs and melons in the summer. Although apples and pears grow in Iraq they are recommended only to lovers of Golden Delicious.

In the current low-tax environment, Baghdad has become a smokers' paradise, with the average packet of cigarettes costing ID500–1,000 (about the same price as one cigarette in the UK and New York). Alcohol is easily available although it can be fairly expensive and the cheap substitutes (such as Garden's Dry Gin) are undrinkable. Even with well-known brand names, bought locally, some report troublesome hangovers and with some makes of cigarette there is a marked difference in taste.

Toiletries are easy to buy and many familiar brands are on sale. Those with delicate hair should bring a supply of shampoo and conditioner, as the local formulas are not always suitable for Western hair. Women should remember to bring a supply of sanitary products, although basics are available from pharmacies in case of emergency.

While basic medication is widely available and inexpensive by Western standards, it often lacks the finesse (and sometimes quality) of drugs bought in the West. Forget chewy, fruity antacids and think crunchy lumps of chalk.

About the only thing that it is still impossible to buy in Iraq is fashionable Western clothing. However, a large number of expensive 'Western' boutiques are springing up around Karrada and some wearable bargains can be hunted down. More importantly, clothing made from 100% cotton is very hard to find and a good supply of cool shirts and trousers is essential for the summer months.

Shopping

SUPERMARKETS

Wurde Karrada-out. Everything from tinfoil to frozen pizza to foreign magazines are all crammed into overflowing Wurde, a favourite among rich Iraqis. One glimpse into the cold cabinet at the bewildering variety of processed cheese and it becomes hard to sustain the notion that it all tastes the same, although fortunately they have a decent selection of foreign cheeses for those who remain unconvinced. The delicatessen counter sells sweetmeats and ready-made traditional foods that are regularly used by Iraqis and provide an easy way to sample local home cuisine. With advance notice the sauces to accompany dishes such as *kubba* can be made up to take away.

Mister Milk Arbataash Ramadan St, Mansour. This legendary store somehow managed to sell imported food throughout the sanctions. Everything is priced in dollars and there is a good range of familiar American and European brands on sale although it can be expensive.

Honey Market 62nd St, near al-Wathaq Sq Masbah. Similar to Wurde, Honey Market aims to sell everything. It is also one of the only places in the city where cuts of pork, bacon and ham can be bought.

B-Town Next to the German Embassy, Karrada-out. This new supermarket, spanning two floors, has a food section downstairs and a small general store upstairs. The food hall has a Western feel with wide aisles and bright lighting, although it doesn't yet have quite the range of the other supermarkets.

Those with a sweet tooth should visit some of Baghdad's famous sweetshops. All the traditional Middle Eastern sweetmeats are available as well as some unique to

Iraq. While they also sell cakes and biscuits, these are exceptionally sugary. **Al-Khassaki** (where the chubby youth on the sign outside is now the shop's owner), halfway down Mansour Street, and **Abu Affif** on Karrada-out are particularly well known. In better times, Iraqis used to visit the **Hamra Hotel** for its patisserie.

ALCOHOL, CIGARS AND CIGARETTES

Cigarettes are available along the side of every road from street-sellers. Some of these are enterprising children who have scraped together enough capital to start their own stall. While rarely street children in the strictest sense, they often help to raise vital money for their families whilst staying out of trouble. If you stop to talk to some of them, you'll be amazed at their precocious business acumen.

A good, if occasionally dry, selection of Cuban cigars can be bought in **Zenobia Tobacco**, on Arasat al-Hindiya.

Alcohol stores are scattered around town, mainly in the Christian areas. There are a number of alcohol shops opposite the Baghdad Tower Hotel on Saadoun Street and a few near the Sheraton, also on Saadoun Street. There is a well-stocked store next to Golden Fingers on Arasat al-Hindiya. Alcohol stores have become the target of attacks – don't dawdle in them.

PHOTOGRAPHS

Developing a normal colour film is inexpensive but photo quality can be very disappointing, and if at all possible serious photographers should aim to have films developed on their return. Developing slide film and having it put into cases can be quite improbably expensive, and again the quality is often very poor, sometimes resulting in heavily scratched slides. Those who decide to have slides developed in Baghdad should make sure they ascertain whether the price includes the cardboard holders. Films, including well-known brands, are available at photo shops; specialist films are harder to find and 36 exposures is the only length available.

Two of the better developers are **Dowali Photoshop** (Kodak sign), on Karrada-out in front of the Hamra Hotel, where two-hour developing costs around US$0.16 per photo and a 36-film costs US$2, and **Kodak**, Saadoun Street, on the right-hand side when driving toward Tahrir Square, a little past the Palestine.

CLOTHES

Traditional dress is sold in the alleys around the Central Bank in downtown Baghdad. At the moment this is one of the less safe areas of the city and extreme caution should be exercised if shopping there. Also, be prepared to haggle vociferously. Alternatively your translator will probably be happy to buy the requisite items for you.

Western-style clothes are available in a number of boutiques on and around Arasat al-Hindiya and Karrada, and most large hotels have a shop selling a few basics. There are a number of shoe shops on Karrada-in, but you should bring sturdy walking shoes with you if required.

Clothes

ELECTRICAL GOODS, SATELLITE PHONES AND COMPUTERS

Karrada-out has become a forest of signs of every size imaginable creating a riot of colour, while satellite dishes, washing machines and microwaves jostle for space on the pavements. Most major electrical bands now have outlets in Baghdad located on or around this street.

While some of these shops sell computers, Sina'a Street, opposite the University of Technology, is still the main place both for software and hardware. Almost any software is available although it will almost certainly be a pirated edition.

Computers are surprisingly inexpensive in Baghdad and the shops on Sina'a Street are happy to custom-build computers and laptops to any specification. A hard drive with more than one fan can be particularly useful in the summer when the death rate among conventional computers can be depressing. While most computer problems can be fixed, be aware that there are no registered repair shops as yet and computer insurance may be invalidated after unofficial repairs.

There are a number of shops selling Thurayas (the local satellite phone company) on Saadoun Street just beyond the al-Alwiyah Club, opposite the petrol station. There is also a big Thuraya dealership on al-Rubayee Street. There are both new and used phones on sale, the price varying according to the country of manufacture and the age. Top-up cards are available from these shops or in most major hotels.

IRAQNA is the mobile-phone provider, based in the Babylon Hotel. Line rental costs around US$12 per month but they require a hefty deposit of around US$500. The connection fee is around US$70, with a handset costing US$120.

MONEY EXCHANGE

Every day the open-air money changers set up their stalls around Firdos Square. When rumours of forgeries among high denominations made ID250 the only note in general circulation, their stalls would be piled high with stacks of banknotes. Often the easiest way to measure the value of a wad of notes was to weigh it, frequently on non-digital scales.

Currency rates are fairly similar throughout the city, although there can be sufficient difference between dealers to make it worth shopping around. If you require large numbers of small-value notes, you may need to hunt for them. There are currency exchange shops everywhere, with a particularly high concentration around Arasat al-Hindiya and on Saadoun Street. All the major hotels have a currency exchange although the rates are invariably dismal.

US dollars are exchanged everywhere and shops will usually exchange pounds sterling, euros and Jordanian dinars without any problems.

SOUKS

The main souks around Rasheed Street in old Baghdad are certainly worth a visit. Although the old covered souks are punctuated by those selling rubber shoes, plastic

THE INTERNET REVOLUTION
Wisam Akram, a computer specialist

Around the globe the computer is seen as a wonderful resource, opening up the world and speeding the completion of tasks. But until last year most people in Iraq had only had bad experiences of computers. Computers held your name on security black lists, army lists and lists that denied exit visas. Computers in government institution were placed in special rooms with large signs proclaiming 'Computer Room – No Entry'. As a result the majority of the population had no idea about the benefits of computers still less about the internet and email. Before the war if you told most people about the power of computers, or about an internet through which you can access the world they would say that you were dreaming or a fool. How could a box do such things?

After Operation Desert Storm communications remained bad in Iraq. There was no international direct dialling and the operator service was slow and erratic. Foreign calls were also expensive. Iraqi people began to feel increasingly removed from the world; even satellite TV channels were banned.

In 2000 a government company launched a limited email service. To open an email account the user had to pay ID100,000, far beyond the budget of almost all Iraqis. The account could only be accessed from a special, monitored centre and for every email sent or received the user had to pay ID1,000. Emails took over two days to arrive.

In 2001 the centre opened an internet service, but the majority of sites were blocked and anyone who wanted to browse the web had to submit his name, ID number, address and pay a large sum of money. At the same time universities were given internet access, but students had to give supervisors the name of all sites that they wished to visit. Later a limited and highly monitored internet service was offered by phone, but few Iraqis could afford or find a computer and the phone lines were so bad that it was useless.

Now after the war everything has changed. All the main streets are lined with internet cafés, the price is good and inside are people of all ages. Many are using cheap web-based voice-lines to talk to distant relatives. Shortly after the war many internet cafés were full of people unable to believe that they were speaking to far-off relatives through a computer. In Baghdad many now carry mobile phones and US$200 will buy a small system to access the web from your house. Day by day Iraqis are rapidly learning about computers and the wonders of international communication. Now Iraqis know the difference between dreaming and awakening.

handbags and endless bolts of gaudy nylon fabric this is where you must come to see Baghdad in action. Herds of jostling women fight over the price of cloth, while trolleys push roughly past, laden with boxes. Hawkers sell cheap wind-up toys and bicycle carts serve hot beans or gooey sweets dripping in syrup. In some areas shoppers have to wade knee-deep in packaging, bubble wrap and shredded paper.

On the other side of Rasheed Street, away from the river, is Shorjah. Filled with stalls selling household wares, many of the alleys are dull with the scent of coffee, spices and the heady aroma of dates.

But it is the traditional souks that retain the ancient magic. The **antique souk**, running along the imposing outer wall of Mustansiriya School, is a series of shops overflowing with finely wrought silver antiques. Although the prices are fairly standard, much of the joy is in browsing, simply to see what bizarre wonders can be rooted out of forgotten corners.

Deeper into the labyrinth is **al-Bazzazzeen**, the textile market. Although this quickly turns into modern fabric stalls, cross-legged tailors in tiny cloth-lined booths can still be seen stitching away in the initial section. It is here that traditional male dress can be bought, from fur-lined woollen capes to cashmere *abaya* seamed with gold.

Diving away from the river and turning back on yourself you come to the **copper souk**. The noise is legendary and deafening as copper pots and decorative platters are hammered into shape. Ornate coffee pots taller than a man leer out of the darkened entrances of several shops, while huge urns and dishes litter the front. Inside these Aladdin's caves are more transportable souvenirs.

Shopping

INSCRIPTION IN A BOOK FROM MUTANABI STREET
The Complete Yes Minister – The Diaries of a Cabinet Minister by the Right Hon James Hacker MP

First inscription on the title page:
'To the Secretary of State for Northern Ireland on the occasion of his birthday, 8th March, 1985'

From the Protection Team

Second inscription on inside cover:
'His Excellency Tariq Aziz'

(signed) Douglas Hurd
Home Office
December 1985

On the other side of Mamoun Street is the **stationery souk**. Although most basic stationery is available in shops more centrally (there is a good shop on Saadoun Street next to Street 45, by the Palestine), this is where to venture if you require anything specific and where university students come to buy their materials.

Souks

Continuing down the stationery souk, it suddenly turns into the **leather souk**. The quality of the leather is high, and although few of the ready-made things would appeal to Western tastes they can make up items to specification. The workshops are in the souk so you can speak to the craftsman and choose the exact leather you want.

On entering the leather souk in the warmer months notice the dramatic drop in temperature. Housed in part of the original Ottoman Souk, with high-vaulted brick roofs, it remains cool even in the height of summer, unlike the modern sections with their plastic roofs.

At the end of the leather souk, you emerge into **Mutanabi Street**. Directly opposite is Shabander café, one of the oldest in Baghdad and the haunt of poets, artists, philosophers and people who like nothing better than to sip tea and discuss their latest thoughts. On Fridays it comes to life as the intellectuals of Baghdad swarm to the **book market** on Mutanabi Street. It is here you will need to come to find reading material.

Browsing among the hundreds of titles lying on the street is one of the weekly highlights of Baghdad and there is always a spattering of Westerners to be found, greedily picking out their week's reading. The range of material available is as astonishing as the number of languages in which it can be found (although the majority of foreign books are in English and French). While bargains are rare those who browse assiduously can find the occasional gem (see box, page 171).

Also on Fridays is the **animal market** in Jumhuriya. While fascinating, it is an unpleasant part of town. Many Muslims look down on those who sell animals and while it is debateable whether the merchants are intrinsically more aggressive or made so by the reception they get, this market does have an unpleasant feel to it and many Iraqis will refuse to take foreigners, particularly women. If you do go, try to keep a low profile and limit lens changes or other conspicuous actions that could draw a crowd. Get out if you feel any change in the mood.

The market itself is both fascinating and harrowing and sells everything from scorpions to Dobermanns although it is predominantly a bird market. Look out for the luminously painted chicks and ducklings, the colour denoting which seller they belong to in case of mass escape. Early in the morning there is a fabulous selection of caged wildlife on display, but by midday little remains and that which does is pitiful. Gasping ducks tied up in the sun slowly baking on red-hot pavements and similarly forlorn rabbits in squalid boxes do little for Western sentimentality.

The fish market is one street in, for those who fancy buying a pet carp or angel-fish.

Souvenirs can be bought in the safety of your hotel, advisable as long as it remains risky to wander the alleys of Old Baghdad. Antiques, jewellery, carpets, paintings and Saddam memorabilia line the foyers of most large hotels. The assortment of odds and ends in each of the almost identical shops of the al-Rasheed Hotel is quite bewildering. Sadly, much on sale in hotels is either very expensive or very tacky and sometimes both.

There is a cluster of antique and carpet shops on Street 45, off al-Saadoun Street, opposite the Palestine Hotel. This road is blocked off, affording these shops some protection and siphoning off the bustle found elsewhere. They have somewhat erratic opening hours, however. There are also several large shops selling antiques and carpets on Salman Faiq.

For those who know what they are buying Iraq is one of the best places to buy **carpets** in the Middle East. The main carpet souk is in Shorjah. You should aim to be able to identify the fibres used and knotting types before committing to an expensive purchase.

Other Practicalities

8

GENERAL INFORMATION

For information on Baghdad or Iraq more generally, go to the Iraqi Assistance Centre (IAC) on the ground floor of the Conference Centre. A team of Iraqi and Coalition Staff do their best to answer any practical questions that you may have about the city, laws, governance etc and are extremely friendly. Unfortunately, their information is sometimes limited or a little out of date. Usually if they don't know the answer they can direct you to someone who does. *Open 08.00–14.00 Sat–Thu.*

The *Official Gazette of Iraq* is published monthly and includes new laws and regulations. Visit www.iraqcoalition.org/regulations/index.html.

PHARMACIES

There are a large number of pharmacies on Saadoun Street, near the statue of Abd al-Muhsin al-Saadoun at the Liberty Monument end. This is the area in which most doctors' practices are located and so there are a wide range of drugs available. They are only open during normal working hours and the area can be somewhat hectic. For chemists selling cosmetics and toiletries as well as medicine, go to Salman Faiq Street (opposite the Mahabar restaurant) or al-Rubayee Street (where there are several), both of which are much quieter areas of town. There is a 24-hour pharmacy in the Sheik Zayed Hospital, near Andalus Square.

The following are well stocked and have English-speaking pharmacists:

al-Shaiklee Pharmacy, al-Kindi St, directly after 8th Street. Open 18.00–21.00, sometimes 11.00–14.00, closed on Fridays and major holidays.

Hunnudi Pharmacy Karrada-in, between 5th and 6th streets from Kahramana Statue. Open 09.30–14.00 and 16.30–18.30, closed on Fridays and major holidays.

HOSPITALS

Every municipality in Baghdad has at least one public hospital. Sanctions coupled with the devastating post-war looting mean that hospitals lack many of the facilities and medicines that the West takes for granted. There is a small fee for entering hospital, and you will be charged for all subsequent treatment and care.

The best public hospitals at the moment are al-Yermouk in Mansour, al-Kindi on Palestine Street in 7th Nissan, and al-Shaheed Adnan on Baba Muadham Street in Rusafa. There is 24-hour emergency care at Shaheed Adnan Hospital in Medical City.

Private hospitals, although more expensive, generally provide better treatment and care. However, none of them has a casualty department, and for non-essential surgery it is still worth travelling to a neighbouring country. The best private clinics in Baghdad are al-Hayat on 52 Street in Karrada, al-Rahebat on Karrada-in, and Karkh Hospital for surgery.

CHRISTIAN SERVICES IN ENGLISH

Anglican St George of Mesopotamia, Haifa Street opposite Meilia Mansour Hotel [4 F5]. There is currently no full-time incumbent, but services are conducted

MARY IN BAGHDAD

Jesus may not be a name you would expect to find in Baghdad, particularly not in the Muslim community, but Esa (the Arabic version), is not uncommon among the Shia. Apart from being an important prophet in Islamic tradition, there is a custom among some Shia women to ask Mary for a child if they are having difficulty conceiving. If they subsequently become pregnant with a boy they will call him Jesus.

Furthermore, in the Koranic Surat 19, the Surat to Maryam, verse 16 says: 'She withdrew in seclusion from her family to a place facing east', and in verse 22: 'So she conceived him, and withdrew with him to a far place'.

There is a strand of thought that interprets these passages to mean that Jesus was born in Baghdad. The location is believed to be where Baratha mosque now stands, on the site of a former monastery. Baratha mosque is on Al-Atehfiya Street near to Sarafiya Bridge.

relatively frequently. It is worth stopping off and asking the exceptionally friendly caretaker when Canon Andrew White is next in town; the caretaker speaks almost no English so bring a translator. Services are in English, with Arabic hymns.

Christian services in English

Catholic St Raphael, Opposite St Raphael's Hospital, 14th St, Karrada-in [4 H6]. Mass is celebrated in English at 17.00 on Sunday. There used to be a mass in French, but this has ceased for the time being due to low attendance. The priest is happy to hear confessions in Arabic, English or French.

EMBASSIES

In the current security situation, diplomatic missions are being kept to a bare minimum. Many missions are also being housed in temporary accommodation. Roadblocks and stringent security checks protect those that remain in town.

For a list of diplomatic missions in Baghdad, see *Chapter 14*.

Consular assistance

British The British mission is in the process of establishing a warden network in Baghdad. They also strongly encourage any British national coming to Iraq to register with them at their offices on the ground floor of the Conference Centre. At the moment there is officially very limited consular assistance provided, although in practice they are doing their best to provide the usual services when the security situation permits. In the light of the FCO travel advice urging British nationals not to visit the country, there are no advice packs available on the city.

USA The US consular office, tel: +1 703 270 0210, on the ground floor of the Conference Centre, has a number of advice sheets available covering a range of topics from medical facilities and pharmacies to adoption regulations. Opening hours are 10.00–12.00,

13.00–16.00, Sat–Thu. Any questions can be directed to email:
asktheconsul@usconsulbaghdad.com or usconsulbaghdad@state.gov.

MINISTRIES

The skyline of Baghdad is littered with bombed, burned, looted and abandoned ministry buildings. Notable only for its pristine condition is the Oil Ministry. Some have been repaired and are once again functioning in permanent accommodation, but the majority have been temporarily reopened in requisitioned buildings.

A list of current locations is to be found in *Chapter 15*.

BANKS

For several months after the cessation of conflict there was no banking system in Iraq and the only way to withdraw more money was to make the tedious trek back to Amman. Out of necessity the majority of foreigners entered the country with huge quantities of hard currency and at least one businessman spent the summer wandering around with the entire liquid assets of his company in his back pocket. Fortunately, many banks are now back in operation and are able to conduct payment and remittance business.

Standard Chartered and HSBC are due to arrive soon: ask when you arrive.

Banks either already approved, or expected to receive approval, by the Central Bank to conduct payment and remittance are, with their points of contact:

Banks

Bank of Baghdad (Mowafaq H Mahmood) Tel: +1 914 822 7083
Credit Bank of Iraq (Fouad M Mustafa) Tel: +1 914 360 0494
Dar Es Salaam Investment Bank (Anwar H Haddad) Tel: +1 914 360 4646
Iraqi Middle East Investment Bank (Abdul Razzak M Ali) Tel: +1 914 360 4242
Commercial Bank of Iraq (Saadoun Kubba) Tel: +1 914 360 4188
Gulf Commercial Bank (Mudher M Hillawi) Tel: +1 914 360 4241
National Bank of Iraq (Ghassan Kamal Jamil) Tel: +1 914 360 2345

Banking hours are normally 08.30–12.30 Sat–Wed, 08.30–11.30 Thu. In winter banks usually stay open half an hour later.

COMMUNICATIONS

The unforgettable ring of the Thuraya and MCI phones is the aural icon of post-war Baghdad. With mobiles finally in town there is now, instead, a riot of new personalised ring tones.

The country code for Iraq is +964, but the international exchange was bombed in the recent conflict and is yet to be repaired. The domestic telephone network is still not fully functional. Although domestic phones work they will connect only to numbers in certain areas.

For a week in the summer a Bahraini network set up an illicit tower in central Baghdad, much to the jubilation of everyone other than the CPA who quickly removed it. Mobile phone connection is finally up, after many months of waiting.

Satellite phones are widely available (see *Shopping* section) in Iraq as are top-up cards. They are prohibitively expensive and the reception is very far from ideal. It is not uncommon to see users craning out of windows or leaping from moving cars in an endeavour to receive an important call. It will be worth buying a satellite for some time if you intend to travel out of Baghdad. Nationwide mobile coverage is some distance away and it is important to retain a means of contact on road journeys.

NGOs, CPA workers and some contractors are entitled to an MCI phone provided free of charge by the CPA. The MCI office is on the ground floor of the Conference Centre. MCI phones used to make both national and international calls; they have become more difficult to obtain and are now limited to national calls only, with a few exceptions.

Due to the relative price of calls, Middle Eastern telephone etiquette is somewhat more relaxed than that of the West, so don't be offended if someone takes a call during a conversation or even in the middle of a meeting.

INTERNET

Under Saddam Hussein there was only a very small number of officially monitored internet cafés that the general public could use (see also box, pages 168–9). They were expensive and access was closely monitored. Since the fall of the regime there has been an explosion in internet usage: sometimes it seems as though there isn't a street in Baghdad without an internet café and often three or four can be found in one building. One of the best is **Sima Satellite** on Karrada-out, particularly in the summer when the icy air conditioning provides sufficient reason to loiter over emails.

One unfortunate side effect of internet freedom is pornography. It is rare to sit down at a public computer without being bombarded with pornographic pop-ups many of which would disturb the most liberal minded. Sometimes the volume of junk springing up on the screen – or there already – renders it impossible to access anything else. This is not uncommon so don't feel embarrassed if you have to ask to swap computers.

By Iraqi standards internet charges remain relatively expensive with an hour costing ID2,000–4,000. Connection speed is infuriatingly slow and servers frequently crash. The major hotels all have internet access, many 24 hour and while it is significantly more expensive (up to US$5 per hour) with printing and other services ridiculously over-priced, the connection speeds are vastly improved and servers generally reliable.

COURIER SERVICES

Insurance policies differ between firms; ask before you send anything valuable.

Aramex Hay al-Wehda District 904, St 6, House 15; tel: 00882166320288; email: Baghdad@aramex.com; web: www.aramex.com. Open 09.00–17.00. Delivery takes around six days. Prices from US$35 to EU/US. There is also an office on the ground floor, Sheraton Hotel.

Other practicalities

DHL Foyer, Hotel Palestine; tel: 001 914 360 6354; email: Tracing.IQ@dhl.com; web: www.dhl.com. Open 08.00–17.00. DHL have daily flights to Baghdad. Delivery takes 2–3 days. Prices from US$80 to EU/US

FedEx Mahala 905, Zukak 1, Bldg 8, Karrada-out St; tel: 008 821 667 771792; web: www.fedex.com. Open 08.00–18.00. Delivery takes 2 days to EU/US. Prices from US$75 to EU/US. There is also a desk on the first floor, Sheraton Hotel (closes at 15.00) and one on the ground floor of the Conference Centre.

Postal service

A new collection of Iraqi stamps depicting ancient forms of transport went on sale for the first time on January 15 2004. The CPA announced in January that 80% of the 275 Iraqi post offices that were operational before the war are again open for business. As yet no one quite knows how long the post takes and the postmaster general is eager for feedback, but you can send letters and packages both internally and internationally (a letter to Basra costs ID500, to send packages overseas costs ID5,000 per pound).

MEDIA

Under the former regime the spectre of the Ministry of Information and Culture dominated the media of Iraq. The legitimate punishment for anyone deemed to have insulted the president, the Revolutionary Command Council, the Baath Party or the National Council was life imprisonment and confiscation of property. Capital punishment was used if the comment was deemed to incite citizens against the state.

Uday Hussein, who became president of the journalists' union in 1992, controlled the media outlets not directly under the ministry's auspices. The interrogation centres that he founded oversaw the disappearance of many journalists, while hundreds more were sent to prison and tortured.

With the ousting of the former regime the number of publications has exploded. Almost all are funded by parties with a political or religious agenda, and the quality of reporting is abysmally low. Of the 230 newspapers currently published in Iraq only 12 are considered to provide well-rounded and objective reporting.

While the newspaper market has exploded, English newspapers are pretty much restricted to *Baghdad Now* published erratically by the 1st Armored Division. It can be bought from street-sellers around the city. International newspapers and magazines are for sale in the major hotels. The only regular independent English publications, the *Baghdad Bulletin* and *Iraq Today*, have both been forced to close as a result of financial difficulties. Archived editions on-line provide a fascinating insight into post-war Baghdad (see websites, page 236).

As traffic jams have increased, so has the need for radio. Popular stations are:

BBC World Service News and programmes. 98 FM
IQ4 Soft Rock. 104.1 FM
Sa'ah Mixture of Western and Arabic pop. 100.4 FM
US Forces 70s' and 80s rock'. 100.1 FM
Armed Forces 107.8 FM. Mixture of popular music.

Most Baghdadis are now addicted to the hundreds of TV channels suddenly made available through satellite. The more expensive hotels provide satellite TV in rooms, although the number of channels actually provided can be depressingly low. If you intend to stay in Baghdad for any length of time make sure you have access to a wide range of channels. Apart from the news stations, MBC2, broadcast from Saudi Arabia, provides a 24-hour diet of American comedy and blockbuster films.

SECURITY COMPANIES

Having increased security is a double-edged sword. While anyone living in a private house should have good, armed security, employing conspicuous guards can, in itself, make you more of a target. Many better areas have developed an impromptu neighbourhood watch and it is certainly advantageous to become part of this if you intend to live in the community.

If you require additional security the following are a selection of companies operating in Iraq, there are many more:

Baghdad-based

ISI (Omar Hadi) Tel: +1 914 360 2492; email: omarhadi@hotmail.com

UK-based

AD Consultancy Tel: +44 (0)8707 070 074; email: security.services@adporta.com; web: www.adconsultancy.com

Control Risks Group Tel: +44 (0)20 7222 1552; email: james.blount@control-risks.com; web: www.crg.com

Genric Tel: +44 (0)1432 379 083; email: nick.duggan@genric.co.uk; web: www.genric.co.uk

Global Risk Strategies Tel: +44 (0)20 7491 7492; email: ops@globalrsl.com; web: www.globalrsl.com

Olive Security (UK) Limited Tel: +44 (0)20 7307 0540; email: barrylb@olivesecurity.com; web: www.olivesecurity.com

US-based

Meyer & Associates Tel: +1 181 742 61199; email: gdesmith@meyerglobalforce.com; web: www.meyerglobalforce.com

RamOPS Risk Management Group Tel: +1 919 740 4597; email: globalservices@ramops.com; web: www.ramops.com

Wade-Boyd and Associates LLC Tel: +1 641 330 4581; email: wbaprotection@yahoo.com

Worldwide-based

Group 4 Falck A/S Tel: +911 242 398 888; email: reg.office@group4falckmesea.com; web: www.group4falck.com

Hill and Associates, Ltd Tel: +85 228 022 123; email: info.ae@hill-assoc.com; web: www.hill-assoc.com

Meteoric Tactical Solutions Tel: +27 126 513 402; email: Juanitavr@bestmed.co.za
Optimal Solution Services Tel: +61 297 555 840; email: optimal1@optusnet.com.au

TRANSLATORS/DRIVERS

Many translators, like drivers, wait by the entrances to major hotels trying to find work. Many are highly qualified professionals desperate to earn some money.

Before hiring someone ask for a recommendation either verbal or written. Don't be pressurised into engaging the first person you meet. Ask around your hotel to see if anyone has a translator/driver they can recommend; this is the safest way of hiring. Try to find out something about their background; if you are at all unsure or things don't seem to tie up then take someone else. Most people strike up an excellent rapport with their translator, but there have been sufficient salutary tales for caution to be exercised. At the moment there is, unfortunately, no respected hiring agency.

NGOS

After the series of tragic attacks against NGO targets many of the large NGOs pulled their Western staff out of Iraq. For those that retain a presence in the country the two main points of contact are the Humanitarian Assistance Coordination Centre – Baghdad (HACC-B), located on the ground floor of the Conference Centre, and NGO Coordination Centre in Iraq (NCCI). The latter prefers to keep their location secret, but HACC-B can provide the relevant up-to-date email address and a point of contact.

NGOs

A list of useful information is available from HACC-B including details of the 12 Civil Military Operation Centres (CMOCs) in Baghdad which serve as 'a one-stop-shop for information for NGOs on a particular neighbourhood in Baghdad.'

At the time of writing there are no longer any NGO security briefings, but NCCI sends out daily security briefs via email.

The Ministry of Planning in association with HACC-B have set up the NGO Assistance Office (also located in the Conference Centre; tel: +1 703 270 0179; email: ngoinfoiraq@yahoo.com). NGOs must register here within 90 days of arrival.

Information and news is provided at web: www.cpa-iraq.org/government/NGO_Assistance_Office/ngo_assistance_office.htm

An exceptionally thorough overview, with a map service, is available from the Humanitarian Information Centre, web: www.hiciraq.org.

Useful websites for NGOs

www.ncciraq.org NGO Coordination Committee in Iraq
www.reliefweb.int Informative daily situation reports
www.iom.int Activity updates
www.unjlc.org Info on routes, access, logistical issues
www.icrc.org ICRC updates
www.irinnews.org Great website, much about NGOs
www.uniraq.org

Other practicalities

BUSINESS

Few large international firms have arrived in Iraq, with most taking a 'wait and see' approach to the security situation. Nonetheless, entrepreneurial individuals of almost every nationality have come in to establish links with Iraqi businessmen, set up partnerships or simply open a business from their hotel room. Amongst some, Iraq is seen as the new Wild West, a country with almost no tax, few rules and much to be won. In all likelihood this will change to some degree, but precisely how remains to be seen.

A 'reconstruction surcharge' of 5% is currently levied on most imports. Personal income tax is capped at 15%.

There is currently no recognised recruitment agency in Baghdad. For businessmen coming to Iraq, the Iraqi Business Centre is a useful initial source of information.

Iraqi Business Centre Ground floor, Conference Centre (Convention Centre); tel: 001 914 360 5113; email: ibc2@baghdadforum.com. A subsection of the Private Sector Development Department, charged with moving Iraq from a command economy to a free-market economy, the Iraqi Business Centre has set up a training facility and runs conferences to introduce foreign businessmen to the ways of doing business in Iraq. They can offer legal advice, such as how to form and register a company. They will also provide lists of Iraqi companies, including profiles and financial information, to businessmen looking for sub-contractors or local partners. In the future they intend to provide updated investment regulations and privatisation news. *Open Sat–Thu 08.30–14.00.*

Useful websites include www.tradepartners.gov.uk and www.i-acci.org, the latter the site of the Iraqi American Chamber of Commerce and Industry. The organisation provides a link between the private sector of Iraq and the rest of the world. The official CPA website has a business section (see *Useful websites*, page 236).

For those requiring up-to-date commercial legal advice, a number of commercial lawyers have set up in Baghdad. Try Ammar Naji, a corporate lawyer specialising in the establishment of entities in Iraq (email: ammarnaji@hotmail.com).

PRESS BRIEFINGS

The **Coalition Press Information Centre** (CPIC) (1st Floor Convention Centre; tel: 001 914 360 5089 email: pressid@baghdadforum.com) will be operating for the foreseeable future, but not indefinitely. Media can gain access to the Convention Centre with their usual ID, but will need to be accredited to attend press conferences and events organised by CPIC. English Applications: Wed/Thu 09.00–12.00; Arabic Applications: Mon/Tue 09.00–12.00. Applicants must bring a valid form of government-issued picture identification (eg: passport), a valid form of press/employee picture ID issued by a media source and a typed and signed letter printed on company letterhead from a legitimate media source stating current employment and requesting that media credentials be issued. Once registered, you will be notified of press conferences and other events via email and receive press releases. Hard copies of the press releases are available to anyone at the desk. Accredited members of the press corps may submit questions, but while those manning the desk are usually friendly and do their best to help, the amount of information they are authorised to give out is extremely limited and you will usually be required to submit an official request. The process is notoriously slow and few requests are satisfactorily answered (via email), especially if you do not have the weight of a major organisation behind you.

Press Conferences organised by the Interim Government are held in the Convention Centre. There is currently no fixed schedule, nor a dedicated press office, but check on arrival. Email iigpmpressoffice@yahoo.com for more information.

The International Press Centre, is also located in the Convention Centre. All the major bureaux operating in Baghdad have desks here.

Museums and Things to See

Despite centuries of war, there are still a surprisingly large number of exceptional sights to visit in Baghdad, some in a near-perfect state of repair (although this is often due to renovation). The main problem is the current security situation. Tragically, many sights are located in the worst areas of Baghdad and should be avoided while the threat to personal security, particularly kidnap, remains high.

If you do venture out to marvel at the wonders on offer be vigilant, try to blend in as thoroughly as possible and do not stand around in crowded streets taking photos and gazing, however tempting that may be. Fortunately in this respect, most of the buildings are almost deserted once inside – it is getting to them that poses the problem. Seek advice on arrival and always take a translator.

MUSTANSIRIYA SCHOOL [map page 212]

Completed in 1234, Mustansiriya School was the first Arab-Islamic university and is among the oldest universities in the world. Built by the 36th Abbasid caliph, Mustansir-billah, the university was unique in its time not only for teaching mathematics, medicine and philosophy in addition to Islamic theology, but also for teaching all four schools of Islamic law. Ibn Battutah, who visited under Sultan Abu Said (1316–35) during the course of his epic journeying, saw fit to comment on the arrangement, noting that each was taught in a separate pavilion complete with its own mosque, but within the confines of one school. Schools traditionally focused on one of the four schools of law: Hanifi, Maliki, Shafei and Hanibali. These are the four main (although not exclusive) approaches to Islamic law, and are named after their founders. All four are still followed today.

At the beginning of the 20th century the school was almost in ruins having served as a caravanserai and then as a river customs. It has now been restored to its former glory.

To enter, walk down the antiques souk (located first right after crossing Shuhada Bridge), keeping the school's wall to your right. On reaching the large wooden gate you must ring the doorbell to gain access. Allow some time as the doorkeeper and his family live at the other end of the building.

Once within the confines of the sanded, palm-filled courtyard it is hard to believe that you have just left a thronging, modern capital. The most notable features of the courtyard are the two sunken arches, or *ewans*, at either end, both framed with exquisite brickwork. Small, dark passages on either side of these lead to lofty classrooms cooled by a series of traditional wind towers and air vents. One end of the school was used to study the Koran, the other the Hadiths. Inside the classrooms, look up at the original brickwork, much of which is blackened, reputedly from the Mongol razing of Baghdad. The rooms leading off the first-floor galleries were student lodgings and study rooms.

A series of signs in English and Arabic point out the major features such as the library that once boasted one of the most important collections in the Middle East, with over 80,000 volumes. As you leave, look above the doorframe where an original wooden beam has been preserved.

Mustansiriya School

Entrance is free, but you should give the doorman a tip. There is a well-stocked gift shop selling books and postcards.

OTTOMAN PALACE [map page 212]

On the other side of Shuhada Bridge from Mustansiriya School (on the same side of the river), the gardens of the Ottoman Palace, or Serail, lead down to the Tigris. Built by Daud Pasha in the early 19th century, the palace quickly fell into disrepair, being later restored by Namuq Pasha in 1851.

The most notable feature is the wide, lofty veranda running round the inner part of the three-sided building. Built in the traditional style, the ceiling consists of a series of narrow beams roughly 0.5m apart spanned by almost imperceptibly arched brickwork.

While structurally undamaged, the rooms are currently a mess of tangled electrical cable, broken marble and polystyrene ceiling tiles – the latter perhaps torn out by an ascetically incensed looter. The gardens are wild, but awash with roses and oleander flowers, with doves cooing in the trees. It was in these gardens that King Faisal I was crowned in 1921.

Set in the garden near the river is the **Kouchela**, or clocktower. Built in 1868 by Madhat Pasha to wake his troops, the inner workings have been pillaged by looters. Fortunately, the finely wrought weather vane, a galleon, proved inaccessible.

The entrance to the Ottoman Palace is at the furthest end near to Maidan Square, reached via a large, black, metal gate. It is not officially open at the time of writing, although it is possible to gain access if you ask permission.

By the entrance is a small section believed to date from the Abbasid period. The echoing dome is entered by a heavily worked archway embossed with large black studs. The small sections of tile panelling on the outside facing the river are worth noting.

ABBASID PALACE [2 F4]

There is some debate both over the date of construction and the building's original purpose. The oldest ruins, discovered in 1900, appear to date from the period of Caliph al-Mahmoun (813–33), but the building seen today is a later construction. Most believe it to be a 'hotel' built by Caliph al-Nasser Lindinillah (1179–1225). Others, most notably the Iraqi scholar Marrouf, claim that it is in fact the remains of the Sharabiyah School, mentioned in Arabic literature. If this is the case, then it was contemporaneous with Mustansiriya School but specialised in Hanibali law.

Beautifully restored, the two-storey barrel-vaulted chambers around a central courtyard are offset by the magnificent 9m *ewan*, the surface finely decorated with intricate brickwork. On the inside of the barrel vaulting, each panel is worked with woven plaster designs.

MIRJANIYA SCHOOL AND KHAN MIRJAN [map page 212]

Much of Mirjaniya School, built by Amin-ed-din Mirjan in 1357, was pulled down in the early 19th century. Mirjan Mosque, famous for its intricate brickwork, is all that remains. Fortunately, some of the elaborately crafted masonry that faced the original structure is housed in the Iraq Museum and survived the looting.

Opposite the mosque is the cavernous Khan Mirjan, which together with other, long-vanished buildings and orchards provided an endowment to the school. This is the only roofed Khan, or caravanserai, in Iraq and provided lodging for merchants as they passed through Baghdad on the many caravan routes to cross the city. Rooms for the merchants lead off a narrow gallery that runs around the inside of the building and is supported by ornate brick arches. Light and air enter through windows in the many-vaulted ceiling, which is 14m high at its apex.

After falling into disrepair, a restoration effort began in 1935. It is currently a restaurant. Khan Mirjan is near the Central Bank in Shorjah.

CALIPH'S MOSQUE [2 G4]

Situated in Shorjah on Khulafa Street, the mosque itself is a recent construction. The minaret, however, dates from 1289 when the original 10th-century minaret was restored after the Mongol invasion. Standing 33m high on a dodecahedral base, the balcony rests on highly decorative corbels. The minaret is known as the Souq al-Ghazil minaret after the nearby spice market.

SHEIKH ABDUL KHADER AL-GAILANI MOSQUE [2 G4]

Originally a school built by Abu Said al-Mubarak, it was later improved and extended by his pupil Abdul Khader al-Gailani (1077–1166), after whom the surrounding area,

Bad al-Sheikh, is named. Hailing from Gail, a town near the Caspian Sea, he founded one of the first *tariqa* (a Sufi ritual system and community), the Qadiriya – still one of the most influential Sufi orders – converted a large number of Jews and Christians, and became known by his disciples as the Supreme Saviour.

The original mosque was destroyed by the Mongols and razed by the Persians. In 1535 the Ottoman Sultan Suleiman the Magnificent rebuilt the mosque. The wide, gently sloping white dome that we see today was of his construction.

In total the complex houses six mosques in varying architectural styles, ranged around a large central courtyard. In the far corner the library houses some exceptional illuminated manuscripts, many of which are on display.

WASTANI GATE AND AL-SAHRAWARDI SHRINE [2 G3]

Travelling along Omar Bin al-Khatab Street, or Army Canal Street, you cannot fail to notice Wastani Gate and the leaning 'tower' of al-Sahrawardi. Whichever direction you are travelling, the view from the raised motorway is depressing. Burning rubbish belching black smoke, the car market, bombed ministries and then suddenly, the crumbling yellow bricks of Wastani Gate on one side and the darker ochre of al-Sahrawardi and the palm-fringed cemetery on the other.

In 892, the Abbasid capital returned to Baghdad from Samarra, continuing to expand on both sides of the river. But it was not until the reign of al-Mustarshid-billah (1118–35) that the first wall was built on the eastern side of the city.

The fortification originally formed a semi-circle stretching from 17th July Bridge

OMAR KHAYYAM (1048–1131 ATTR)

> Awake! for Morning in the Bowl of Night
> Has flung the Stone that puts the stars to Flight:
> And Lo! the Hunter of the East has caught
> The Sultan's Turret in a Noose of Light.

While studying under Imam Mowaffak in Naishapur, Omar Khayyam became a close friend of Nizum al-Mulk and Hassan Sabbah. Perhaps recognising each other's brilliance they made a remarkable pledge here described by Nizum:

One day Hassan said to me and to Khayyam, 'It is a universal belief that the pupils of the Imam Mowaffak will attain to fortune…let us make a vow, that to whomsoever this fortune falls, he shall share it equally with the rest, and reserve no pre-eminence for himself.' 'Be it so,' we both replied.

to Jumhuriya Bridge and punctuated by four gates: Mu'adham, Wastani (or Dhafariya), Halaba and Basaliya. Wastani is the only gate to survive. Mu'adham and Basaliya Gates fell foul of the construction and later extension of Rasheed Street and Halaba Gate was destroyed by the Ottomans in 1917.

Wastani Gate consists of a crennelated cylindrical tower 14.5m high, crowned by an octagonal dome. Two splendid gates lead to walled bridges over what was

It was to Nizum that the obligation fell, becoming Vizier to the Sultans of Baghdad, Ap Arslan and later Malik Shah. Hassan became a courtier while Khayyam, bent on studies in mathematics and science, received a stipend and when Malik Shah decided to introduce a solar calendar Khayyam was one of eight astronomers designated with the task. The result far surpassed any contemporaneous system and was more accurate than the later Gregorian calendar (1 day in 3770 years vs 1 in 3330). His mathematical acumen was no less astounding; he was the first to discover the binomial theorem and his work on cubic equations was significant in the development of algebra.

Whilst in office, Nizum built the famous Nizimiya School in Baghdad. Hassan fell from grace as a courtier and went on to found the notorious Assassins, a terrorist organisation that would later decapitate Nizum on the road to Baghdad.

once the moat. You can climb to the top of the gate by way of a parapet running along each wall, which also enables a closer inspection of the complex star design in the masonry above the main gate.

Both the gate and a section of the wall are under reconstruction in an effort to rebuild them. Unfortunately neither the materials nor the workmanship lives up to the original.

The listing tower of **Sheikh Omar al-Sahrawardi's Shrine** is a landmark of Baghdad. Built in 1225 it is, strictly speaking, a conical dome in the Seljuk style and is one of the oldest buildings in the city. The courtyard of the mosque frames the contrasting minaret and dome against the sky, one a brightly tiled column the other a monochrome but layered complexity. From the surrounding cemetery, with its traditional arched tombs, the outer walls of the shrine are punctuated with ornate tile work, the honey-colour of the bricks and clay accentuated by the deep blue sky.

A Sufi of Iranian decent, the actual tomb of al-Sahrawardi is crafted from wood and silver and lies directly beneath the dome. In stark contrast to the imposing catafalque, an unadorned alcove in one wall houses a rock-hewn coffin, supposedly belonging to Musta'sim-billah, the last caliph of Baghdad.

SITT ZUMURRUD KHATUN'S TOMB (ZUBEIDA) [1 E4]

Behind the central station, in a now neglected cemetery, lies the tomb of Zumurrud (Emerald) Khatun, mother of Caliph al-Nasser Lindinillah. It was built under her instruction at some point before her death in 1202. An octagonal Seljuk dome surmounts a hexagonal mausoleum, the external surface of which is faced with panels of intricate brickwork.

Of similar design to al-Sahrawardi's Shrine, but with fewer tiers in the dome, Zumurrud's tomb is an enchanting place, made all the more so by the dereliction of the surrounding area and the feeling that you have sprung upon something unvisited. The brickwork on the base is worth a visit in itself, but it is the inside of the mausoleum that captivates. Zumurrud's austere stone tomb stands in the centre of the hollow structure. On the stark, whitewashed inner walls traces of henna handprints can be seen, the visual reminder of vows pledged within. Unlike the dome of al-Sahrawardi, the ovoid constituents of each tier are pierced to let in a shaft of light, the bright Iraqi sun turning them into a myriad burning eyes focussed toward the tomb. Stand directly beneath the dome in the height of the day and look up into the apex of the dome and the complex interplay between shadow and light becomes a dizzying kaleidoscope. Popular myth holds it to be the tomb of Zubeida, the wife of Harroun al-Rasheed, who died in 831 and is in fact buried in the Qureish cemetery in Kadhimiya.

IMAM AL-ADHAM MOSQUE [1 D2]

Abu-Hanifa, over whose shrine the current mosque is built, was one of the great Sunni Imams and founder of the Hanifite school of law, followed by around 53% of Sunni Muslims worldwide.

Abu-Hanifa (699–767) lived through the reign of ten Umayyad caliphs, but it was in the reign of Mansour, second Abbasid caliph and founder of Baghdad, that his disdain for politics caught up with him. When the Caliph asked him to become Grand Quzi, or Judge of the Empire, Abu Hanifa refused, saying he was unfit for the position. Supposedly the caliph, taken aback, shouted, 'You are a liar!', to which Abu Hanifa promptly retorted, 'You have merely proved my point, a liar is not fit to be Grand Quzi.' For his disobedience Abu Hanifa was thrown into gaol where he died, reputedly from poison.

Historical texts claim 50,000 people joined in the recitation of his first funeral prayer, and the shrine attracted such attention that a small settlement grew up around it. In 1066 the Seljuk leader renovated the shrine, built a large dome and founded a Hanifite school in the precincts.

Over the centuries the shrine has been repeatedly rebuilt and renovated, the current design dating from the early 1970s when the building was extended. The many-vaulted honeycomb interior is worth seeing for the overwhelming plasterwork, with tiny sections painted in a muted riot of pastel colours. A silver grille surrounds the tomb of the Imam.

KADHIMAIN SHRINE [1 C1]

The shrine at Kadhimiya is one of the main holy Shia shrines. Built on the old Qureish Cemeteries, two of the 12 Imams are buried within: Musa al-Kadhim, the seventh Imam, and his grandson, Muhammad al-Jawad, the ninth Imam.

The installation of Musa al-Kadhim as seventh Imam marked the first sectarian split within the Shia community. Ja'far al-Sadiq, the sixth Imam, had intended that his eldest son, Ishmael, inherit the role from him. When al-Sadiq was poisoned by Caliph al-Mansour in 765, Ishmael had already died, and instead his second son Musa became Imam. Whereas the majority of Shia believe that Ali's line ended with the occultation of the twelfth 'hidden Imam' in 934 and accept Musa as the seventh, others claimed that Ali's line had ended with the death of Ishmael. The Ishmaelis, or Seveners as they came to be known, were politically highly active, in marked contrast to the rest of the Shia community of the time.

After 14 years in prison, Musa al-Kadhim is believed to have been poisoned by Harroun al-Rasheed in 818, who then displayed his body to prove to the population that he had not been occulted (ie disappeared from human view, with the assumption that he would return again in the future). Muhammad al-Jawad became the ninth Imam on the death of his father, at the hands of Caliph al-Mahmoun. He befell a similar fate, poisoned by Caliph Mu'tasim in 835 at the age of 30.

The original 10th-century shrine was destroyed by the Mongols. The current shrine dates from 1515, consisting of two gilded domes and four minarets set in the midst of a walled courtyard.

The traffic around the shrine is impossible, leaving little option but to fight your way through the narrow alleys and souks leading to the shrine. On the final approach stalls selling religious souvenirs abound; Ali mugs and plates, Ali T-shirts, religious CDs, sweet sellers and photographers persuading pilgrims to pose for a personalised memory of the visit.

At the entrance women, who must wear an *abaya*, undergo a security check. The ferocious jostling behind the screen can be somewhat alarming, so try to bring a female translator. It is possible to borrow an *abaya* from the security desk if you cannot find one elsewhere. Once inside men and women can reunite within the courtyard, but are once again separated within the shrine.

A visit to al-Kadhimain can be an almost overwhelming visual experience. The inner surface of the arched external gateways are lined with gold and framed with

Kadhimain Shrine

vivid tiles, the gates made of heavily carved wood. Within, the walls of the courtyard are again tiled with floral and vine motifs, their colours softened by age and a layer of dust to a tumbling of muted blues, greens and reds, offset by gaudily painted columns.

Entering through towering doors plated with delicately etched silver panelling, you'll find the shrine itself is literally dazzling. The fluted walls are covered in a mosaic of mirrors, flashed with shards of azure glass, the light glancing from the myriad different angles. A wooden clock and the darker painted dome look strangely out of place amid the shimmering walls and the gold and silver of the tombs.

ROYAL CEMETERY [1 D2]

Purpose-built for the royal family, the lofty tri-partite mausoleum is set in its own well-tended gardens, the green tiled onion-dome visible from some distance. King Faisal I and his wife are buried in one wing, kings Ghazi and Faisal II in the opposite wing. At the base of each fluted section are the names of the princes and princesses of Iraq.

The Royal cemetery is in Adhamiya.

BRITISH CEMETERY [2 F3]

This well-looked-after cemetery is opposite the Turkish Embassy in Wazeriya district. Sand-coloured headstones mark the final resting place of hundreds of members of the British Army who fell during World War I, and afterwards. The inscriptions on most are still clearly visible, some are very moving. Special memorials commemorate the Muslim, Sikh and Hindu soldiers who died.

In the centre of the cemetery, surrounded by pink-flowering oleander, is the mausoleum of Sir F Stanley Maude who conquered Baghdad in March 1917 and died later that year from cholera (see box, page 18).

The cemetery is kept locked, but the groundsman is happy to show you around. There is no official entrance fee, but you should tip him appropriately.

The British Civil Cemetery is on Nidhal Street. Gertrude Bell's grave is to be found there (see box, pages 214–15).

SASSOON PALACE [1 E3]

Built in 1908 by Shahoul Shashooah, the 'Palace' is now a private house, although the current owner is often happy to show visitors around if you ask in advance.

Between 1921 and 1926 King Faisal I took the house as a residence, but the pavilion and much of the grounds were destroyed in the floods of 1927–28. The last Shashooah to live in the house was Lady Farha Shashooah who finally sold the property in 1933.

Today it provides a picturesque glimpse into the past. The rooms and furnishings are original and although the current owner is Muslim there are still traces of the house's Jewish past for those who know where to look, especially on the furniture and crockery (the best Baghdadi furniture was made by Jewish craftsmen).

For those interested in old photographs there is a fascinating collection of images, both of the political élite and of everyday life from the first half of the 19th century.

One particularly interesting feature of the house is the cellar with a small pool fed by the Tigris.

The Sassoon Palace is at number 22 Corniche Street in the Kissrah area.

Jewish architecture abounds in Baghdad, particularly in Betaween, where many traditional houses are still standing. Look for the Star of David, particularly over doorframes and on the underside of balconies.

MUSEUMS
Iraq Museum

Al-Alawi St, Midan Hathaf; web: http://info.uibk.ac.at/c/c6/c616/museum/museum.html [2 F4]

No-one quite seems to know how many of the priceless treasures were taken from the Iraq Museum in the post-war looting. The initial estimate came in at 3,000-4,000 including 47 major pieces, although later articles claimed that the majority had been returned by museum employees who had taken them home for safekeeping. The alarming truth is that we may never know. Although the museum is closed, probably until 2005, in order to complete extensions and catalogue all the items that remain, many of the important pieces had exact replicas, and it remains possible that many of the items returned were in fact not the originals. The irreplaceable Sumerian collection was particularly targeted.

Fortunately the Assyrian friezes and huge winged sphinx proved impossible to move, leaving at least one gallery intact.

The Iraq Museum is opposite the Bunia Mosque, near to the Central Station.

Script Museum

140 Haifa Street, opposite the old British Embassy [map page 212]

The Script Museum normally has a rotating display of around 50 works at any given time, although this has been halted until the security situation improves. With a collection of around 43,000 scripts and manuscripts dating back several hundred years, there are some stunning illuminated works on vellum, including a range of Korans, from verses written on a single grain of rice to tomes as large as a table, ancient books on anatomy to historical epics. To view manuscripts not on display, you must apply to the script department of the Iraq Museum. The Script Museum is currently searching for new premises. *Open 08.00–14.00.*

Baghdad Museum

Shuhada Bridge Street, Rusafa [2 F4]

The concept behind the Baghdad Museum, a series of montages from everyday Baghdadi life in bygone times, provides an insight for those interested in the roots of the local culture. Scenes include the liver-griller, the circumciser, the depilator and the arcane 'Broad Bean She-Seller'. Unfortunately, the dummies and scenes are often so badly put together that the result is more hilarious than informative.

'Women at a traditional wedding' look as though they have just stepped off the set for *Saturday Night Fever* and the accompanying booklet, although interesting, has gems such as 'Women were performing the duties of physicians, prescribing remedies and poisons and killing people.' That said the room displaying old photographs of Baghdad is fascinating.

Founded by Gertrude Bell (see box, pages 214–15) and housed within a large merchant's house in the traditional style, the building itself is worth seeing, especially the brickwork in the central courtyard and the cool underground sleeping quarters which would have protected the family from the summer heat. The museum originally held the items now found in the Iraq Museum, opening in its current form in 1970. *Open 09.00–18.00*

CHURCHES

There are numerous churches in Baghdad, most concentrated in Karrada and around Masbah. While most are of no particular architectural merit, they are fascinating for their denominational diversity: Syrian Orthodox, Armenian Orthodox, Armenian Catholic, Syrian Catholic and Chaldean, in addition to the denominations more familiar in the West. The Syrian churches all conduct some services in Syriac, the Edessene dialect of Aramaic, the language spoken by Jesus.

One of the oldest churches, the Syrian Orthodox Church of the Virgin Mary in Maidan Square, Rasheed Street, is built around an earlier Nestorian church. Restored in the 17th century, little remains of the original.

MARTYRS' MONUMENT [2 J4]

The split dome of the Martyrs' Monument is one of the landmarks of the eastern half of the city. Built by Mitsubishi in 1983 to commemorate the Iraqis who died in the eight-year Iran–Iraq war, the original idea was to cover the two halves in gold leaf, a burning 40m-high memorial to the dead. Fortunately, the Japanese engineers noticed the flip side: the inside of the domes would focus reflected light and roast anyone who visited the monument in summer. Instead the deep aquamarine, glazed tiles of the Ishtar Gate in Babylon were chosen as a model.

The monument is one of serenity, the cool blue and clean lines of the dome offset by a series of lakes around the sweeping marble court. The fountain in the centre represents the tears of the relatives. The museum contains a moving if bizarre collection of miscellaneous and mundane objects belonging to the dead.

MONUMENT TO THE UNKNOWN SOLDIER [4 F6]

Originally a huge arch in Firdos Square, the new monument, built in 1982 and weighing over 550 tonnes, is near the victory arch and former Republican Palace. Looking out over the Palace complex from the roof of the Sheraton, the Monument to the Unknown Soldier looks like a huge UFO about to land. Apparently the artist, Hisham Munir, found inspiration from an inverted bowl resting at an angle, and it symbolises a traditional shield dropped by the dying grasp of an Iraqi warrior. At the moment the monument is within the Green Zone, so you will have to be accompanied by a suitably authorised resident.

VICTORY ARCH [4 F6]

The famous crossed swords are a celebration of Iraq's victory over Iran, according to the official outcome. The hands are modelled on Saddam's and were cast in the Morris-Singer foundry in Basingstoke. The swords, cast in Iraq, were supposedly made from the melted-down weapons of the dead. The two arches are now in the Green Zone.

Suggested Day Tours

10

Before doing any significant walking in Baghdad you should check the current security situation. Even when the situation permits, you should aim to keep as low a profile as possible, don't stop to take photos in public, always have a local guide with you, don't carry any valuables and cover-up. Women have the additional advantage of being able to wear local clothing, which should be seriously considered if you want to spend the day on foot.

Although the majority of shootings have not been random opportunistic crimes, there was the tragic case of a British journalist shot outside Baghdad Museum and there is no reason to believe that the risk is no longer there.

While the threat of kidnap remains, foreign nationals should avoid all unnecessary exposure.

OLD BAGHDAD – A WALKING TOUR

Start early. Old Baghdad is deserted after dark and you should certainly not be walking in the area after 16.00, earlier in winter.

By car cross Jumhuriya Bridge and look up at the arches; the green and white square is the 3rd ID insignia painted over the original portraits of Saddam. Turn right on to Haifa Street. On your left you will pass St George's Anglican Church followed by the burnt-out remains of al-Rasheed Theatre. Although the damage from the outside appears immense the stage and seating is still in perfect condition. On your

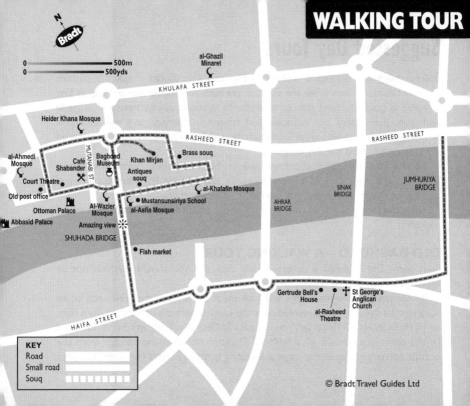

WALKING TOUR

N

Bradt

| 0 | | 500m |
| 0 | | 500yds |

KHULAFA STREET

al-Ghazil Minaret

Heider Khana Mosque

RASHEED STREET

RASHEED STREET

al-Ahmedi Mosque

Café Shabander

Baghdad Museum

Khan Mirjan

Brass souq

MUTANABI ST

Antiques souq

Court Theatre

Old post office

al-Khafafin Mosque

Ottoman Palace

Al-Wazier Mosque

Mustansunsiriya School

SINAK BRIDGE

JUMHURIYA BRIDGE

Abbasid Palace

al-Asfia Mosque

AHRAR BRIDGE

Amazing view

SHUHADA BRIDGE

Fish market

HAIFA STREET

Gertrude Bell's House

al-Rasheed Theatre

St George's Anglican Church

KEY
Road
Small road
Souq

© Bradt Travel Guides Ltd

left shortly after the al-Rasheed Theatre and opposite the Melia Mansour Hotel is a large house in the traditional Baghdadi style. This is the house of Gertrude Bell (see box overleaf). A family is living in the grounds but they are happy to let you look around, although the floor has collapsed in places and the walls are daubed in *fedayeen* (foreign fighters who came to support Saddam) graffiti. Continue along Haifa Street until you reach Shuhada Bridge. If the security situation permits, the walking tour should commence here.

After skidding your way through the bustling fish market spilling over most of the pavement before the bridge, cross over to the other side of the river. The view of Old Baghdad from the apex of the bridge is possibly the best in Baghdad. On your left are the Kouchela (clock tower) and the Ottoman Palace, to the right rise the high brick walls of Mustansiriya School. The beige of the bricks and the tawny river is relieved by green palm trees and the many coloured domes and minarets that pierce the skyline.

Once over the bridge take the first right, just after al-Asfia Mosque, where Sufi sheikh al-Muhasabi is buried. The antique souk is on your left and the outer wall of Mustansiriya School on your right. The school is entered from the large sunken gate.

Continue on past the school and enter the covered cloth souk. On your right you will come to al-Khafafin Mosque. The minaret is the oldest in the city. Although heavily restored over the centuries, parts of the original Abbasid structure remain. Built by Zumurrud Khatun, it dates from before her death in 1202. Turning left, plunge deeper into the souk, before turning back on yourself. After walking through the modern

GERTRUDE BELL (1868–1926)

Educated at Oxford, where she was the first woman to gain a first in history (after only two years of study), Gertrude Bell's passion for travel and adventure soon got the better of her. She travelled widely in Europe, made two round-the-world tours, gained renown as an Alpine mountaineer and finally fell in love with Arabia and its peoples.

Many of the trips that she made deep into the Mesopotamian desert and mountains accompanied by Bedouin tribes showed not only a remarkable adaptability to local customs but an intrepid resilience and determination that earned her the enduring respect of those peoples. They called her a 'daughter of the desert'.

Her meticulously kept diary meant that she had the most comprehensive geographic knowledge of Mesopotamia, and her travels left her with a shrewd

material market you will come to the brass souk on your right. Walk down this clammering alleyway until you reach Rasheed Street, and then turn left. Turn left again when you reach Shuhada Street. Baghdad Museum is then on your right.

Further down the street turn right into the stationery souk. As the stationery souk turns into the leather souk, al-Wazier Mosque, built in 1660, is on your left. On either side of the entrance to the mosque there are staircases leading up to the idea of who was likely to be a friend or foe of the British. As a result she was the only woman drafted into the Arab Bureau as an intelligence agent. In 1921 Winston Churchill gathered together a group of 40 Middle East experts to decide the fate of Mesopotamia. Miss Bell was the only woman invited.

Many of the current borders of Iraq were drawn up by Gertrude Bell and she was instrumental in choosing Faisal as the new king of Iraq, remaining his closest advisor for the rest of her life. She is also remembered for founding the Baghdad Archaeological Museum.

Her letters home and diary entries provide a fascinating first-hand account of the political tensions of the British Mandate as well as in-depth descriptions of the customs, practices and lifestyle of the various tribes of Iraq.

Complete transcripts of her letters and diaries can be read at www.gerty.ncl.ac.uk/home.

gallery level of the souk from where you can observe the bustle below and inspect the brickwork above.

At the end of the souk is Mutanabi Street, with the famous café Shabander on the corner in front of you. The building on your left is the Ottoman Palace. Opposite the main entrance to the palace is the court theatre, recently restored. The bricks used in the restoration were the traditional *fershi* bricks; notice the difference between these and other buildings in the area that have been restored using cheaper, modern materials. To gain access to the Ottoman Palace walk to the square at the end of the street where, on your left, is a large, black gate.

On the other side of the square is the old British Post Office, still complete with red pillar-box. It houses a post office museum, but it is closed at the time of writing.

Standing in the square the highly patterned, glazed dome of al-Ahmedi Mosque towers above a low street. The buildings are in the traditional style with fabric awnings draped across the street. Unfortunately, it is inadvisable to take this route to the mosque. Instead take the main road leading toward Rasheed Street; an antique shop is on the corner housed in an imposing traditional house. Once back on Rasheed Street, turn left. It is here that many of the traditional cafés are found and groups of men can be seen huddled around hookahs drinking tea. On your right is the mosque of Heider Khana, built by Daud Pasha. The brickwork on the outer wall is particularly impressive.

Crossing over Rasafi Square, Khan Mirjan will be on your right near to the Central Bank. This is the perfect place to take a late lunch away from the bustle of the streets.

Time: 2–4 hours

SHRINES AND MOSQUES – BY CAR

Starting early head to the tomb of Sheikh Sahrawardi. Wastani Gate is on the other side of the motorway and is also worth a visit. From there drive to Sheikh Abdul Khader al-Gailani Mosque. There is a car park nearby and some interesting old houses. Drive down Khulafah Street; the ancient minaret of the Caliph's Mosque near the al-Ghazil Souk is one of the finest examples of original brickwork in Iraq.

Take the riverside road to Adhamiya, perhaps stopping off at the Sassoon Palace if it takes your interest.

In Adhamiya pause at the green-domed royal cemetery, before going to Imam al-Adham Mosque. It is worth visiting this Sunni shrine the same day that you visit the Shia shrine of al-Kadhimain; the contrast is marked and not dissimilar to the difference between many Protestant and Catholic churches in Europe.

Opposite the clocktower in Imam al-Adham Mosque is a small car park spanning the main road running alongside the mosque and a smaller road that joins it. Take this smaller road following it around an s-bend. Here are to be seen some of the finest examples of traditional Baghdadi houses in the city. In excellent condition whole streets are still made up of original buildings complete with wooden facing and closed-in wooden balconies; some of the lanes are so narrow that the upper storeys of the houses almost touch.

Cross the river by either Aimma or Adhamiya Bridge. Traffic in Kadhimiya is horrific, especially near to the shrine. It may be better to walk through the souk, although the pressing crowds are perhaps more daunting than the traffic. Women must wear an *abaya* and be searched to enter the courtyard of Kadhimain Shrine. If you are running out of time, al-Kadhimain can be visited on the way to Samarra.

From Kadhimiya make your way to Mansour. Although access has been closed off you can drive around Jama al-Rahman. Located on the former site of Mansour racetrack it is still under construction, although progress has been halted. Nonetheless, the basic edifice is complete and the sheer enormity of the squat and many-domed structure is awe-inspiring. Saddam was in the process of building a still larger mosque, to be the largest in the world, but only a few supports have been completed. These are nonetheless sufficiently lofty for the mind to boggle at the scale of the intended building.

On the return to central Baghdad, stop off at Sitt Zumurrud Khatun's tomb, located behind the central station.

Time: Dependent on traffic

Al-Shaheed Mosque

Suggested Day Trips

11

In a country as full of archaeological treasures as Iraq it can be difficult to know what to visit if time is limited. There are many sites of interest an easy day trip away from Baghdad. A small selection follows. The local security situation and road status should be ascertained before any visit.

AGARGOUF

These are remains of the ancient town of Dur-Kurigalzu, founded by Kassite King Kurigalzu in the 15th century BC on the Sumero-Babylonian plan. The ziggurat has been rebuilt to the top of its base/platform and the adjoining palace complex has been similarly restored.

The massive ruins of the ziggurat tower 57m over the surrounding plain, the utter silence and majestic solitude punctuated only by flocks of birds nesting in the brickwork. While the ziggurat bares little resemblance to its original form (only the inner core remains) its sheer size and age leave the viewer breathless, with each brick still clearly visible.

The ziggurat survived due to a clever method of construction; after every seven or eight rows of bricks comes a layer of rope and matting, protecting the structure from seepage, damp and cracking.

Agargouf lies approximately 30km from central Baghdad. Turn right off Highway 1 at Abu Graib Bridge and follow the road for about a kilometre. The signpost for the lane to Agargouf is on your left, directly after the road passes over a railway track. The site is currently desolate, though under normal conditions there is an entrance fee of ID1,000 and it is a favourite picnic spot.

CTESIPHON

Around 30km south of Baghdad, past the huge nuclear site bombed by Israel in 1981, is the modern town of Salman Pak. Salman Pak was one of the close companions of the Prophet Mohammed and the first Persian to convert to Islam. There is a gilded shrine in the centre of the town.

The city of Ctesiphon was founded on the east bank of the Tigris in around 144BC, by Parthian king Mithradate I. On the opposite bank was Seleucia, a city founded in 301BC by a successor of Alexander the Great. This meeting of cultures continued relatively peaceably until Avidius Cassius destroyed Seleucia in AD165.

In AD628 Ctesiphon, by then the capital of the Persian Sassanid Empire, was ravaged by the Byzantine armies. Only nine years later the victorious Arabian forces vanquished the Persians in the battle of Qadisiya and called the area *Mada'in* or 'The Cities'.

Among the ruins of Ctesiphon, dating from the 2nd century BC, is the largest single-span brick archway in the world: 37m at its apex and spanning a distance of 25.5m, its clean arc and yellow brickwork are particularly photogenic against a clear blue sky.

The nearby **Qadisiya Panorama** is described in the official Iraqi guidebook as 'the most recent after the Panoramas of Moscow, Leningrad, Belgium and North Korea. It is a great sight, nationally and historically, a work achieved by the Iraqis in the days of the national liberation hero Saddam Hussein.' Little now remains of the 1640m² panorama after it was destroyed in the post-conflict looting.

On the way back from Ctesiphon it is only a short detour to **Tell Harmel**, located in the middle of a residential area in Baghdad Jadida. Turn right just after Sina'a Bridge. After meandering round residential streets, dodging children and potholes you suddenly come upon the salt-covered site. Although you can drive around the fence, the restored priest's house affords a raised view over the city, once the administrative capital of the Eshnunna Kingdom (around 1850BC) and the layout of the city can be clearly seen.

Clay tablets unearthed from here include the Eshnunna Laws that predate Hammurabi's Code by around two centuries and a tablet bearing Euclid's theorem, anticipating his solution by around 1700 years.

SAMARRA

In AD836, Mu'tasim-billah, son of Harroun al-Rasheed, moved the Abbasid capital to Samarra. The capital returned to Baghdad only 56 years later, but the remains of this brief heyday are breathtaking.

The highlight of a trip to Samarra is the **Melwiya**. This extraordinary structure, 52m high and 33m wide at its base, resembles an old-fashioned helter-skelter, the pinnacle reached by a 2m-wide stairway that winds round the outside. Built as the minaret to the **Grand Mosque** (the remains lie next to it) the view from the chamber at the top is awe-inspiring although the dizzying climb is not advisable for anyone suffering from vertigo.

A few kilometres away is the **Caliph's Palace**. From the outside little of human origin seems to remain in the rocky, pitted landscape, save a small unpromising entrance. This, however, leads down into a web of underground passages that open up into vaulted chambers, before suddenly bursting into a vast, sunken, open-air courtyard. Only the tacky replastering of the interior mars this fascinating warren of a palace.

The **Palace of the Belovèd**, or Ashuk Palace, has also been rebuilt in places, bricks praising Saddam Hussein peppering the walls. A huge, fortress-like building, the view from the upper chambers looks over the pampas plains below.

In the heart of Samarra is a gold-domed Shia mosque, **Ali Hadi**, the resting place of the 9th and 10th Imams. The 12th Imam, Muhammad al-Mahdi, was occulted in Samarra.

At the time of writing Samarra, 135km northwest of Baghdad and one of the towns within the so-called Sunni Triangle, has seen significant amounts of political unrest. All monuments are daubed with pro-Saddam graffiti. While tourists receive a rapturous welcome at the major sights, extreme caution should be exercised, especially if you go into the town itself.

BABYLON

The famous basalt 'Lion of Babylon' is original, though little else of note is. Although the site of Babylon dates back to Akkadian times (around 2350BC), the reconstruction work has focused on the Babylon of King Nebuchadnezzar (late 7th

BABYLON

How many miles to Babylon?
Three score miles and ten.
Can I get there by candlelight?
Yes, and back again.
If you heels are nimble and light
You'll get there by candlelight.

A children's nursery rhyme

Babylon is around 70 miles from Baghdad. One of the ancient initiation rites for wizards was to find the Haroot and Maroot caves in Babylon and walk there by candlelight. After sleeping in the caves they were to return home, again by candlelight.

century BC). The unrecognisable ruins of his summer palace can be seen, now little more than a pile of bricks. Several vaulted structures have been posited as the remains of the hanging-gardens, one of the Seven Wonders of the Ancient World.

Babylon is 90km south of Baghdad near to Hilla.

Babylon

KARBALA

There are three shrines at Karbala, those of Hussein, Abbas and Owan, Hussein's cousin. The mosque, which houses Hussein's shrine, is built on the site of the battle of Karbala. Hussein, Ali's second son, and a band of loyal followers were surrounded by the troops of the Umayyad caliph, Yazid I (680–83), at Karbala and massacred. Hussein was the last to fall, cradling his infant son as he died. His death became symbolic to the Shia both of the injustice of the world and the impossibility of combining religion and politics.

Restored to its former glory after the Wahabbi attack and destruction of 1802, the golden domes and minarets of Karbala can be seen from some miles away. Hussein's tomb is encased in silver and the walls surrounding the mosques are covered in beautiful ceramic tiles. The most notable feature of Abbas' shrine is the silver gateway.

Karbala, 80km southwest of Baghdad, is the second most important of the Shia holy cities, after Najaf. **Najaf** is slightly too far from Baghdad for a comfortable day trip (180km), although with an early start it is possible.

Language

12

ARABIC PHRASES

Linguistic notes

- The vowels in bold are long (in Arabic these are usually the long vowels written into the script, short vowel sounds are usually omitted when writing)
- The words used below are a mixture of fus'ha (classical Arabic) and regional and local dialect. Those used should be understood by people in Baghdad.
- Arabic has sun and moon letters. The moon letters are basically: a, b, f, g, h, k, m, p, q, v, w, y (this is a crude description because letters do not equate exactly and there are other letters with similar sounds to the above in Arabic). For the foreigner the main importance of sun and moon letters comes with the use of the definite article 'the' or 'Al-' in Arabic. Before a moon letter the l is pronounced so al-Hamra, as written. Sun letters drop the l so al-Sadr is pronounced as-Sadr.

Yes	*Na'am/A'ee*
No	*La*
Good Morning	*Sabah alkhier*
Good Evening	*Masa'ah alkhier*
Hello (standard greeting)	*A-salaamu aleekum*
Welcome	*Ahlaan/Marhaber*

How are you?	*kaif-Alhaluka* (response: *zayn, shukran*)/*Kaif a-haal* (response: *al-hamdu lilah*) *Shloonik?* (response: *shakbaarik*)
I am well	*jaed/zeen*
Good bye	*ma a-salaamah*
Please	*ruja'in*
Thank you	*shukraan*
Do you have…?	*hul anduk?*
What is your name?	*ma ismek?*
left	*yusar*
right	*yameen*
straight ahead	*amam/gubal*
back	*khalf*
stop	*towaqaf*
How much is….?	*kem asa'ar*
250	*maetaan wa hamsuwn*
500	*hamsumae*
750	*sabuma'a wa hamsuwn*
1,000	*elf*
half	*nusf*
0	*sufr*

1	*waahed*
2	*ithnaan*
3	*thulaathah*
4	*arba'ah*
5	*khamsah*
6	*sittah*
7	*saba'ah*
8	*thumaaneeah*
9	*tisa'ah*
10	*'ashrah*
11	*aahed 'ashur*
12	*ithnee 'ashur*
o'clock	*saa'ah*
tea	*shaaee*
coffee (without sugar)	*qahooah bidoon sukr/shakr*
coffee (medium sugar)	*qahooah sukr/shakr qaleel*
coffee (lots of sugar)	*qahooah sukr/shakr ketheer*
bread	*hubs*
cheese	*jibn*
meat	*lahm*
vegetables	*khudar*

Arabic phrases

fruit	*fairkiha/fuwakeh*
without meat	*bedoon lahm*
delicious	*latheeth*
more [food/drink]	*almezeed*
come on/let's go	*nedheb/ yalla*
yesterday	*albaarihah*
today	*aleeoom*
tomorrow	*bukra/ba-cher*
everyday	*kuleeoom*
journalist	*suhafee*
aid worker	*a'amal musa'id*
businessman	*rajuul a'amaal*

STREETS AND SIGHTS IN ARABIC
Hotels and apartments

al-Andalus Apartments	شقق الأندلس
al-Dulaimi Apartments	شقق الدليمي
al-Mosafer Apartments	شقق المسافر
al-Rabie Apartments	شقق الرابي
Aghadir Hotel	فندق اغادير
al-Gader Hotel	فندق القادر
al-Hamra Hotel	فندق الحمره

Language

al-Masbah Palace Hotel	فندق قصر المسبح
Andalus Palace Hotel	فندق قصر الاندلس
Babylon Hotel	فندق بابل
Baghdad Tower Hotel	فندق برج بغداد
Cedar Hotel	فندق الارز
Flower Land Hotel	فندق ارض الازهار
Hamurabi Palace Hotel	فندق قصر حمورابي
Hotel al-Finar	فندق الفنار
Hotel Atlas	فندق اطلس
Hotel Ishtar Sheraton	فندق عشتار شيراتون
Hotel Palestine	فندق فلسطين مرديان
Janatadan Hotel	فندق جنة عدن
Kandeel Hotel	فندق قنديل
Karma Hotel	فندق الكرمة
Mansour Melia Hotel .	فندق المنصور ميليا
Orient Palace Hotel	فندق قصر الشرق
Rimal Hotel	فندق رمال
Sadeer Hotel	فندق السدير
Sebel Hotel	فندق سبيل
Sumer Land Hotel	فندق ارض سومر

Streets and sights in Arabic

Restaurants

La Coquette	مطعم الحسناء
Coral Beach	مطعم شاطي المرجان
Legend Restaurant	مطعم الاسطورة
Pizza Reef	مطعم بيتزا الريف
La Terrasse	مطعم الشرفة الزرقاء
White Palace	مطعم القصر الابيض

Navigation points

German Embassy	السفارة الالمانية
Iraq Museum	المتحف العراقي
National Theatre	المسرح العراقي

Main streets, squares and bridges

Abu Newas Street	شارع ابو نواس
Arasat al-Hindiya Street	شارع عرصات الهندية
Canal Street	شارع القناة
Haifa Street	شارع حيفا
Jadriya Street	شارع الجادرية
Jamiya Street	شارع الجمعية
Karrada-in	كرادة داخل
Karrada-out	كرادة خارج

Language

Masbah Street	شارع المسبح
Nidhal Street	شارع النضال
Palestine Street	شارع فلسطين
Rasheed Street	شارع الرشيد
Rubayee Street	شارع الربيعي
Saadoun Street	شارع السعدون
Salman Faiq Street	شارع سلمان فائق
Sinak Bridge	جسر السنك
Shuhada Bridge	جسر الشهداء
Jumhuriya Bridge	جسر الجمهورية
Kahramana Square	ساحة كهرمانة
Andalus Square	ساحة الاندلس
Aqba bin Nafi Square	ساحة عقبة ابن نافع
Firdos Square	ساحة الفردوس
Tahrir Square	ساحة التحرير

Babylonian inscription

Streets and sights in Arabic

Further Information

FURTHER READING
General introduction

Bates, Daniel and Rassam, Amal *Peoples and Cultures of the Middle East,* Prentice Hall, New Jersey (1983).

Dickson, Mora *Baghdad and Beyond,* Dobson Books, London (1961).

Docherty, J P *Let's Visit Iraq,* Macmillan, London (1988).

Hourani, Albert *A History of the Arab Peoples,* Faber and Faber, London (2002).

Armstrong, Karen *Islam: A Short History,* Weidenseld and Nicholson History (2001).

Lewis, Bernard *The Crisis of Islam: Holy War and Unholy Terror,* Random House, London (2003).

Lovejoy, Bahija *The Land and People of Iraq,* J B Lippincott, New York (1964).

Mansfield, Peter *The Arabs,* Penguin Books, London (1992).

Munier, Gilles *Guide de l'Irak,* Jean Picollec Editeur (2000).

Richard, Thames *Let's Go to Iraq,* Franklin Watts, London (1989).

Visual Geography Series *Iraq in Pictures,* Sterling Publishing, New York (1970).

Young, Gavin *Iraq: Land of Two Rivers,* Collins, London (1980).

Baghdad

Alexander, Constance *Baghdad in Bygone Days,* John Murray, London (1928).

Basmachi, Dr Faraj *Treasures of the Iraq Museum,* Ministry of Information, Baghdad (1976).
    Available (with special permission) at the Iraq Museum.

Beck, Sara and Downing, Malcolm (eds) *The Battle for Iraq BBC News Correspondents on the War against Saddam and a New World Agenda*, BBC Worldwide, London (2003).

Coke, Richard *Baghdad: The City of Peace*, Butterworth, London (1927).

Daily Telegraph, *War on Saddam*, Robinson, London (2003).

Hiro, Dilip *Secrets and Lies: Operation 'Iraqi Freedom' and After*, Nation Books, New York (2004).

Horwitz, Tony *Baghdad Without a Map*, Dutton, New York (1991).

Le Strange, Guy *Baghdad during the Abbasid Caliphate*, London (1924).

Omaar, Rageh *Revolution Day: The Human Story of the Battle for Iraq*, Viking, London (2004).

Pax, Salam *The Baghdad Blog*, Atlantic Books, London (2003).

Ramesh, Randeep (ed) *The War We Could Not Stop: The Real Story of the Battle of Iraq*, Faber and Faber, London (2003).

Ria, Milan *Regime Unchanged – Why the War on Iraq Changed Nothing*, Pluto Press, London (2003).

Roberts, Paul Willian *The Demonic Comedy – the Baghdad of Saddam Hussein*, Mainstream Publishing, Edinburgh (1999).

Simpson, John *The Wars Against Saddam: Taking the Hard Road to Baghdad*, Macmillan, London (2003).

Warren, John and Fethi, Ihsan *Traditional Houses in Baghdad*, Coach Publishing House, Horsham (1982).

Wiet, Gaston *Baghdad: Metropolis of the Abbasid Caliphate*, University of Oklahoma Press, Oklahoma (1971).

Further reading

Ancient kingdoms

Cottrell, Leonard *Land of Two Rivers*, Rockhampton (1963).

Dalley, Stephanie (ed) *The Legacy of Mesopotamia*, Oxford University Press, Oxford (1988).

Kramer, Samuel Noah & the editors of Life Books *Cradle of Civilization*, New York (1967).

McCall, Henrietta *Mesopotamian Myths*, British Museum Press, London (1990).

Roux, Georges *Ancient Iraq*, Pelican Books, Hammondsworth (1966).

Art and culture

Baram, Amatzia *Culture, History and Ideology in the Formation of Ba'thist Iraq*, Macmillan in association with St Anthony's College, Oxford (1991).

Michell, George (ed) *Architecture of the Islamic World*, Thames and Hudson, London (1978).

Osborne, Christine *Middle Eastern Cooking*, Prion Books, London (1997).

Roden, Claudia *The Book of Jewish Food*, Viking, London (1997).

Salim, Nizar *Iraq Contemporary Art* (Vol 1– Painting), Sartec, Lausanne (1977).

Stevens, E S *Folk–tales of Iraq*, Oxford University Press, Oxford (1931).

Modern Iraq

Aburish, Said *Saddam Hussein: The Politics of Revenge*, Bloomsbury, London (2000).

Al–Khalil, Samir *Cruelty and Silence*, Penguin Books, London (1994).

Al–Khalil, Samir *Republic of Fear*, Hutchinson Radius, London (1989).

Al–Khayyat *Honour and Shame: Women in Modern Iraq*, Al Saqi Books, London (1990).

Batatu, Hanna *The Old Social Classes and the Revolutionary Movements of Iraq* Princeton University Press, Princeton, NJ (1978).

Childs, Nick *The Gulf War*, Wayland, Hove (1988).

Clarke, Ramsey *The Fire This Time*, Thunders Mouth Press, New York (1992).

Coughlin, Con *The Secret Life of Saddam*, Macmillan, London (2002).

Dempsey Amy *The Life & Times of Saddam Hussein,* Parragon, Leeds (1996).

Goodman, Susan *Gertrude Bell*, Berg Women's series, Leamington Spa (1985).

Haj, Samira *The Making of Iraq, 1900 – 1963,* State University of New York Press, New York (1997).

Hiro, Dilip *Iraq, A Report from the Inside*, Granta Books, London (2003).

Jabbar, Faleh *Why the Intifada Failed in Iraq since the Gulf War: Prospects for Democracy,* CARDRI (Committee Against Repression and for Democratic Rights in Iraq), Zed Books, London (1994).

Khadduri, Majid *Independent Iraq – A Study in Iraqi Politics since 1931*, Oxford University Press, Oxford (1951).

Kimball, Lorenzo *The Changing Pattern of Political Power in Iraq, 1958 – 1971*, Robert Speller and Sons, New York (1972).

Metz, Helen *Iraq: A Country Study*, Library of Congress, Washington (1988).

Penrose, Edith and E F *Iraq: International Relations and National Development*, E Benn, London (1978).

Simons, Geoff *Iraq: From Sumer to Saddam,* MacMillan, London (1994).

Simons, Geoff *Iraq: Primus Inter Pariahs, a Crisis Chronology 1977–98*, Macmillan, London (1999).

State Organisation for Tourism *Iraq*, Baghdad (1982). Available in several languages.

Tripp, Charles *A History of Iraq*, Cambridge University Press, Cambridge (2000).

Travel in Iraq

Dabrowska, Karen *Iraq: The Bradt Travel Guide*, Bradt, 2003

Mackintosh, Tim (ed) *The Travels of Ibn Battutah*, Macmillan, London (2002).

Stark, Freya *Baghdad Sketches*, Murray, London (1947).

Wallach, Janet *Desert Queen: The Extraordinary Life of Gertrude Bell*, Phoenix Giant Paperback, London (1996).

USEFUL WEBSITES

www.geocities.com/iraqinfo/index.html?page=/iraqinfo/sum/baghdad/baghdad.html

www.cia.gov/cia/publications/factbook/geos/iz.html Sections on Iraq.

www.baghadadbulletin.com and www.iraq-today.com These sites provide archived articles mainly focused on Baghdad providing local perspectives.

www.iraqcoalition.org and http://iraq.usembassy.gov/ Current and archived official information from the CPA and new sovereign Iraq.

www.globalsecurity.org/military/world/iraq Maps, history, politics, defence.

www.bbc.co.uk/news Has an indepth 'Iraq in Transition' section including profiles of key figures.

Foreign Liaison Offices in Baghdad

Australia House 5, St 5, Babylon District, Jadriyah; tel: 778 22 10/25/15/01

Austria House 38, St 30, Sect 929, Hay Babil; tel: 008737 61353867 / 0088216 63220370; fax: 008736 1353869 / 0088216 63220372; email: auttrade@uruklink.net

Czech Republic House 11, St 37, Sect 601, Hay Al-Mansour; tel: 0088216 63225192; fax: 008717 62142621

China Room 1404, Sheraton Hotel; tel: 008737 6179871

Denmark Room 909, al-Rasheed Hotel; tel: 008737 6179871 / 0088216 54201717 / 001 914 360 6595

France House 7, St 55, Sect 102, Abu Nawas; tel: 008737 62724066 / 001 914 822

Germany House 40, St 2, Sect 929, Hay Babil; tel: 008706 00207995 / 001 914 360 4295; fax: 008706 00249552

Greece House 63, St 13, Sect 913, Hay AL-Jadriya; tel: 008733 82026514 / 0088216 21442162 / 001 914 360 5438; fax: 008733 82026515

Hungary Sect 609, Hay Al-Mutanabbi; tel: 0088216 51103187; email: huembag@mailbox.hu

India House 6, St 25, Sect 306, Hay Al-Adhamiya; tel: 0088216 63225179

Italy House 33, St 15, Sect 304, Hay Al-Magreeb; tel: 008736 822201445 / 001 914 360 4073; email: delegazione.baghdad@esteri.it

Japan House 50, St 21, Sect 919, Hay Babil; tel: 0088216 51120195 / 008737 61213234 / 001 914 360 0284; fax: 008737 61213235

Netherlands House 10, St 38, Sect 103, Hay Al-Nidhal; tel: 008737 62953523 / 0088216 51157359 / 001 914 360 3943; email: bag@minbuza.nl

Pakistan House 14, St 7, Sect 609, Hay Al-Mansour; tel: 0088216 89801745 / 001 914 360 4612; email: pakembbag@yahoo.com

Poland House 22/24 , St 60, Sect 904 Hay Al-Wahda; tel: 008737 62053413 / 0088216 63226174; fax: 008737 62053415; email: poltrade@tlen.pl

Portugal House 24, St 4, Sect 609 Hay Al-Mansour; tel: 008707 63070770 / 001 914 360 5954

Russian Federation House 4, St 5, Sect 605, Hay Al-Mansour; tel: 008737 63006658 / 001 914 360 5443/44; fax: 008737 63006660; email: russian_embassy_in_iraq@land.ru

Spain House 1, St 3, Sect 609, Hay Al-Mansour; tel: 008737 61316659

Sweden House 15, St 11, Sect 803, Hay Al-Andalus; tel: (Amman) 00962 6 5931177/5930178/5930494; fax: 00962 6 5930179

Switzerland House 41, St 5, Sect 929, Hay Al-Babil; tel: 004131 3241871; fax: 004131 3241872

Turkey House 7, St 1, Sect 301, Hay AL-Wazirya; tel: 008737 62632035 / 001 914 360 5567

United Kingdom Green Zone; tel: 008707 63572961 / 001 914 360 7842

United States Convention Centre; tel: 001 914 360 6306/1025

International organisations

European Commission House 53, St 11, Sect 609, Hay Al-Mansour; tel: 001 914 822 9148

United Nations House 53, St 11, Sect 609, Hay Al-Mansour; tel: 0088216 33333661

Ministries

Ministry of Education (التربيـــــــة) [1 E2/2 H4] Antar Sq, the old Educational Training Institute/Ministry of Oil

Ministry of General Labour (الاشـــغال العامـــة) [CC] Near Quasir (Al-Sindbad) Hotel, near Ahmedi Mosque

Ministry of Agriculture (الزراعة) [4 H5] al-Andalus Sq

Ministry of Communication (الاتصـــــالات) Near Iraqi Airways, behind Al-Rahibat Hospital off Kahramana Sq

Ministry of Culture (الثقافـــــة) [4 K5] Iraqi Fashion House, Palestine St

Ministry of Displaced and Immigrated Persons (المهـــاجرين والمهجـــرين) [4 G6] Qasr Jumhuri St (GZ)

Ministry of Electricity (الكهربـــاء) [2 H4] in Ministry of Oil

Ministry of the Environment (البيئـــة) [4 H5] Next to Sheik Zaid Hospital

Ministry of Finance (الماليـــة) [2 G3] Palestine St, near Turkmen Club in former headquarters of Electronic Computer

Ministry of Foreign Affairs (الخارجيـــة) [4 F5] Next to al-Rasheed Hotel, 22 April St

Ministry of Health (الصـــحة) [2 F3] Bab al-Muadam, behind the former Ministry of Defence

Ministry of Higher Education (التعليـــــم العـــالى) [4 H/J5] St 52, Karrada, opposite Immigration Office

Ministry of Housing and Construction (الاعمـــار والاسكان) [4 H5/4 F5] Near al-Farooqa General Company, behind Ibn Al-Nafeer hospital/Yafa St

239

Ministry of Human Rights (حقـــوق الانســان) [3 E5] Opposite Zawra Park, next to Engineers' Union, by former Air Force HQ and Institute of Fine Arts

Ministry of Industry and Minerals (الصـــناعة والمعـــادن) [2 G4] Behind Liberation Monument, near Armenian Church

Ministry of the Interior (الداخليـــة) [2 H4] College of Police, near Shaab Stadium

Ministry of Justice (العـدل) [CC] By former Saddam Art Centre, Near al-Ahrar Bridge

Ministry of Labour and Social Affairs (العمـــل والشـــؤون الاجتماعيـــة) [2 G2] Palestine St, al-Bakr University for Military Studies

Ministry of Municipalities and Works (الاشـــغال والبلـــديات) [2 F4] Near Shuhada Bridge

Ministry of Oil (نفـــط) [2 H4] Palestine St and Port Said St

Ministry of Planning (التخطيـــط) [4 H5/4 H7] al-Quds School for Computer, Sq 52, near the Italian Hospital/Arasat al-Hindiya

Ministry of Science and Technology (العلـــوم والتكنولوجيـــا) [4 F7] al-Jadriya, near Baghdad University

Ministry of Trade (التجـــارة) [2 H4] In Ministry of Oil

Ministry of Transportation (النقـــل) [4 F5] Opposite Alawi Garage

Ministry of Water Resources (المـــوارد الماليـــة) [2 J4] Near former Olympic Committee

Ministry of Youth and Sport (الشـــباب والرياضـــة) [3 E5] Planetarium, Zawra Park

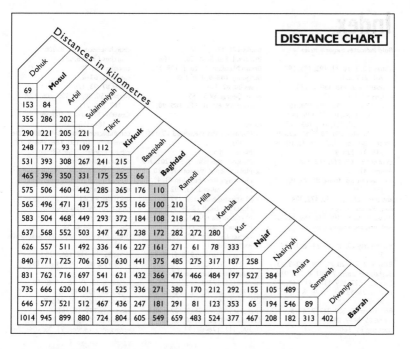

Index

Index

Central Baghdad across the River Tigris (GH)

Insert Ctesiphon (CA)

Shrine with market scene in foreground (GH)

Insert Ziggurat Agargouf (CA)

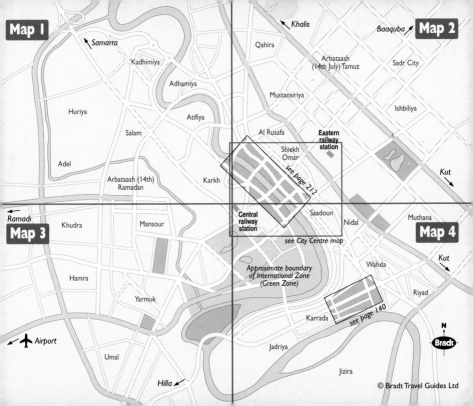

see page 212

see City Centre map

see page 140

Map 1

Map 2

Map 3

Map 4

Samarra

Kadhimiya

Adhamiya

Atifiya

Huriya

Salam

Adel

Arbataash (14th) Ramadan

Karkh

Al Rusafa

Shiekh Omar

Eastern railway station

Central railway station

Saadoun

Khalis

Baaquba

Qahira

Arbataash (14th July) Tamuz

Sadr City

Mustansiriya

Ishbiliya

Kut

Ramadi

Khudra

Mansour

Nidal

Muthana

Hamra

Yarmuk

Wahda

Kut

Approximate boundary of International Zone (Green Zone)

Riyad

Airport

Karrada

Umal

Jadriya

Jizira

Hilla

N

Bradt

© Bradt Travel Guides Ltd

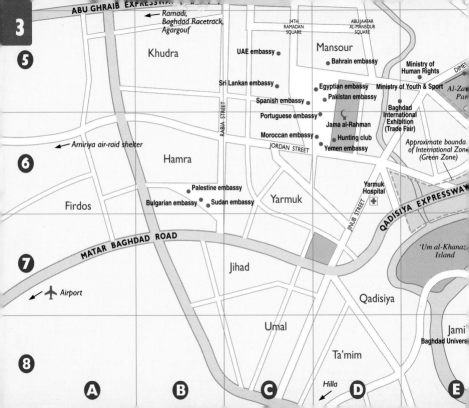

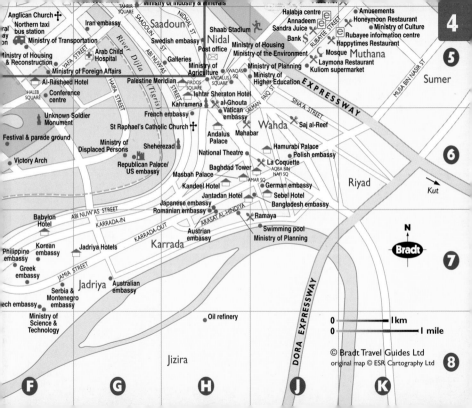

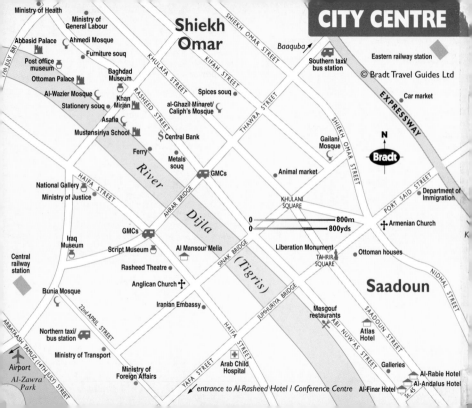

Ministry of Health
Ministry of General Labour
Abbasid Palace
Ahmedi Mosque
Furniture souq
Post office museum
Ottoman Palace
Al-Wazier Mosque
Stationery souq
Baghdad Museum
Khan Mirjan
Asafia
Mustansiriya School
Central Bank
Ferry
Metals souq
National Gallery
Ministry of Justice
GMCs
Iraq Museum
GMCs
Script Museum
Central railway station
Rasheed Theatre
Al Mansour Melia
Anglican Church
Bunia Mosque
Iranian Embassy
Northern taxi/ bus station
Ministry of Transport
Ministry of Foreign Affairs
Arab Child Hospital
Airport
Al-Zawra Park

Shiekh Omar
Sheikh Omar Street
Kifah Street
Spices souq
al-Ghazil Minaret/ Caliph's Mosque
Thawra Street
Baaquba
Southern taxi/ bus station
Eastern railway station
Car market
Expressway
Gailani Mosque
Animal market
Shiekh Omar Street
Port Said Street
Department of Immigration
Armenian Church
Khulani Square
0   800m
0   800yds
Liberation Monument
Ottoman houses
Tahrir Square
Saadoun
Masgouf restaurants
Atlas Hotel
Galleries
Al-Rabie Hotel
Al-Andalus Hotel
Al-Finar Hotel

Khulafa Street
Rasheed Street
Haifa Street
River
Dijla
Afrak Bridge
Sinak Bridge
(Tigris)
Jumhuriya Bridge
Haifa Street
Yafa Street
22nd April Street
Arbataash Tamuz (14th July) Street
15th July Bri
Saadoun Street
Abi Nuwas Street
Nidhal Street

© Bradt Travel Guides Ltd

Bradt

entrance to Al-Rasheed Hotel / Conference Centre